HÖTTLLAND

PART II

A LIFE AFTER DEATHS

Keith Lowry

Paperback – ISBN 978-3-00-051568-2

CONTENTS

Höttl: 1983
"The Americans had systematically looked for experts."

The Alt Aussee Höttl returned to in the winter of 1947 was not the enclave he had left two and a half years earlier. Gone was the furor that had engulfed much of Ausseerland prior to the German collapse, replaced by a semblance of its former tranquility. As a result, news of Höttl's imminent return quickly became sustenance for the town's thriving rumour mill, generating discussion amongst early morning patrons at village shops, as well as robust debates around the evening *'Stammtisch'*. About to re-enter a milieu of varying political constituencies, Höttl faced the problem of determining when and where to project the appropriate persona. The idea of re-cycling the image of the well-intentioned, betrayed nationalist, so useful in previous circumstances, had been made more difficult by revelations of Nazi atrocities at the war crimes trials. Hoping to avoid closer scrutiny over some of his own more questionable activities, Höttl attempted to initiate his own rehabilitation.

Höttl: 1999
"I never had to face a court...either German or Allied... I was never charged. I was of course arrested because of my rank and position... for investigative purposes. But the examiners soon realized that I was an 'anständiger Mensch', (upstanding person),... and I was exonerated by an American court and released... Furthermore, the Allied authorities de-Nazified me, as they called it. I was also exonerated from an Austrian court because they knew that I did not participate personally. That I believed in it for as long as I did is my own fault. You know the German phrase, 'mitgefangen, mitgehangen'. That is absolutely obvious."

While the claim of having never faced a court of law was technically correct, Höttl had in fact been charged and sentenced. The offence in question stemmed from his membership in the *"Schutzstaffel der Nationalsozialistische Deutsche Arbeiterpartei"*, (SS) committed two weeks shy of his nineteenth birthday in March 1934. The SS, as well as the Nazi Party itself, had been declared illegal by the War Crimes Tribunal, *'by reason of their aims and the means used for the accomplishment thereof*', and Höttl's rank and status had made him liable for prosecution and a lengthy jail term. The sentence handed down in Nuremberg however, was significantly shorter than that meted out to others of equal rank, fuelling speculation that a deal had been cut in exchange for betraying former comrades.

Now back in Alt Aussee, Höttl not only wanted to avoid being branded a turncoat or traitor, but also keep knowledge of his new assignments as obscure as possible. As much as his ego may have yearned to boast of his latest undertaking, doing so would have ruined his ability to gather information. As a result, only a select few residents were informed about his new status, one of them, Fritz Fischer. The decision to confide in Fischer was largely a result of Fischer's own reported recruitment by the American Counter Intelligence Corps (CIC), which had installed him as head of a meat delivery service, as a cover for keeping tabs on certain people within Ausseerland. Fischer's connection to Höttl was thought to have begun in the summer of 1945, when the pair met at the Glasenbach POW camp near Salzburg. Fischer was released in early 1946, and returned to Alt Aussee to develop a close relationship with the rest of the Höttl family, facilitated by the fact his sister was a close friend of Höttl's wife, Elfriede (Friedl). Given the stark conditions that existed after the war, Fischer claimed it was simply the urge to lend a hand to a fellow neighbour in need that had drawn him to help the family. As the months went by, the connection gradually deepened, eventually coming to include visits to the Höttl household two or three times a week, frequent enough for the children, Hagen 8, Völker 5, and Andrea a mere six months, to reportedly look upon Fischer as an ersatz father. As life can be in small towns, the regularity of Fischer's calls did not go unnoticed by others in the community, and it wasn't long before rumours about the nature of the *'friendship'* began to emerge. Asked about the conjecture in 1999, Fischer brusquely dismissed speculation about an affair. Whether merely being chivalrous or not, his proximity to Elfriede had likely provided the opportunity to learn details about Höttl's imminent return, as well as his plans to work with the CIC. As both men were later reluctant to discuss their work together, little is known about dealings they had following Höttl's return. As a result, one can only surmise why despite having a well-paid job and a network of family and friends in the area, in mid - 1948, Fischer abruptly left Alt Aussee for Germany, never to return. Asked in 1999, whether his departure had anything to do with veiled threats Höttl was rumoured to have uttered against him, Fischer bluntly denied a connection, making it clear he had no intention of further discussing the subject.

On the afternoon of December 19th, 1947, amidst an atmosphere of curiosity, suspicion and indignation, residents of Alt Aussee were treated to the spectacle of a flashy new Mercedes chauffeured into town by Höttl's old colleague and driver Ottokar Pessl. It was not the most subtle of entrances and quickly swelled rumours over the source that sponsored it. Over the next few weeks other displays of ostentatiousness followed, including sightings of Höttl's strutting through town in a full length canary-yellow leather coat. Although such behaviour would have created misgivings in whatever town Höttl chose to live in, the fact it was occurring in the region where the legend of Nazi gold had had its genesis only served to increase speculation as to the origin of Höttl's suspected 'wealth'. For a time it seemed as though every resident of the village had his or her own private hypothesis. One rumour that saw considerable circulation insinuated Höttl need not concern himself with earning an income because of the money, bonds and gems he had smuggled out of the Balkans during the war. A second rumour maintained his friend and colleague, Austrian industrialist Fritz Westen, had rewarded his 'partner' to the tune of 600,000 Schillings, for aiding in the transfer of 'mobile machinery' from Yugoslavia to Austria shortly before the end of the war. A third enduring tale centred on the belief Höttl was living on funds from secret accounts established on his three 'peace' trips to Switzerland, a rumour that gained support when a French memorandum, revealing the names of individuals sought in connection with properties confiscated from the Jews, was sent to to CIC headquarters in Salzburg. Not only was Höttl's name on the list, but also an attached hand-written notation stating that "*very few people know that Höttl was responsible for the transfer of Kaltenbrunner's assets into Switzerland.*" Of all the stories focused on Höttl's alleged prosperity at the time, the most credible was one that referred to remnants of Operation Bernhard. According to this theory, Höttl was 'known' to have had access to a large cache of counterfeit pounds shortly before the end of the war, time enough it alleged, for a portion to have been deposited in secret accounts in Switzerland.

Also woven into the numerous beliefs on Höttl's livelihood, was the claim he was supporting himself from donations supplied by a number of

Hungarian Jews he purportedly helped escape to Switzerland in 1944. A similar assertion had been rolled out at Nuremberg in 1945, as part of Höttl's strategy to focus attention on what he claimed were his noble, if not always successful, humanitarian efforts towards the Jews.

Höttl: 1945

"At some point in June 1944, I made the acquaintance of a Dutchman by the name of Jaac van Harten, an agent from the Joint Distribution Committee. He asked for my intervention on behalf of certain Jewish families in Budapest, to exclude them from the evacuation and to secure false passports for them to travel out of the country. I was partly successful to get immigration visas into neutral states, Sweden, and Turkey, and so on, for those people. I worked together with Harten all of the time in Budapest, but as soon as the Jewish action had been extended into Budapest, and he being a Jew himself, was endangered by it, I brought him into Meran, near the border between upper Tyrol and Southern Italy."

In 2001, Völker Höttl bolstered his father's claim, saying the people in question had been so grateful for the actions Höttl had taken on their behalf, they volunteered to testify for him at Nuremberg the following year. That Höttl had the authority to obtain the documents and authorizations necessary to save individuals from the hands of Eichmann's henchmen was never in question. The question left open for many residents of Alt Aussee, was why he hadn't used such influence to intervene more often or much earlier. Authentic rescuers had been active since the 1930's, whereas most of the self-proclaimed Samaritans had only rallied to the cause in late 1944 or early 1945, often in an attempt to cloud their previous activities.

Despite the fact Höttl's tenure as a CIC operative had barely begun, concern over his reported extravagance was great enough to prompt a brief internal investigation by CIC officials. Unable to find any concrete evidence tying him to illicit or donated wealth, investigators chose not to take any action, citing 'real politic' and a compromise between *"justice and utilitarianism"* as the basis for their decision. For the majority of Alt Aussee residents however, the mystery of how Höttl was supporting himself and his family remained. With the exception of Fritz Fischer, few at the time had been aware of his financial arrangements with the CIC. Material culled from CIC annals, shows that beginning in 1948, Höttl's estimated CIC earnings had been between 10,000 and 14,000 Austrian shillings a month, a substantial sum for the time and circumstances. As conspicuous and disturbing as Höttl's style of dispensing those funds may have been for some, it was anything but impetuous. For someone about to embark on a recruitment drive for informants, it was a shrewd method of *'impressing'* the type of people he was seeking to engage.

Located at the northern tip of a scenic lake, where the Alps give way to the hills of central Austria, it was to the city of Gmunden that Höttl was ordered to report in early 1948. According to most accounts, he needed little time to adjust to his new base of operations, immediately throwing himself into the job of recruiting staff, *"with conviction and ambition"*. His efforts in that arena were aided by the fact that up until then, Austria had only managed to institute a meagre facsimile of what could be called a de-nazification program. It should be said however, that Austria's laxness towards prosecution had not been discouraged by the occupying powers. As a result of that lacklustre performance, numerous ex-Nazis had been allowed to return to a normal life, unhampered and unchallenged by their dubious pasts, providing a pool of people Allied officials could use to further their own agendas. In the western half of the divided country for example, the Americans appeared willing to turn a blind eye to past endeavours, when it came to selecting people to help establish a stable and functioning democratic alternative to the Soviet-backed administration already in place in Vienna. As part of an overall policy designed to discourage the Soviets from trying to expand their own zone of influence further west, a great degree of leniency was shown when scrutinizing the resumés of prospective candidates.

Harry Rositzke, CIA operative:
"We knew what we were doing. It was absolutely necessary that we make use of every bastard. The most important thing was that he was an anti-Communist"

Told to abide by what were less than stringent recruitment guidelines, Höttl quickly realized the leeway he would have in selecting his own operatives. One of the first to be inducted into the nucleus of his fledgling network was former SS Major Erich Knud Kernmayer. Born in Graz on February 27th, 1906, the 42 year old journalist had been friends with Höttl since their days together in Vienna. A leading member of the Young Socialist Workers before *'finding'* National Socialism, Kernmayer had participated in a Trotsky Communist youth movement, an escapade which at first glance would appear to have disqualified him for consideration by the CIC. No objection was raised however, when Höttl recommended he be appointed as his director of operations. Instead, the Americans simply accepted the explanation that Kernmayer's youthful experience with the Trotskyists had in fact served to transform him into just the sort of rabid anti-Communist they were seeking. Following his ritual passage through the Austrian 'Studentenbunden', Kernmayer had signed up with the rapidly expanding Austrian NSADP. Arrested for illegal Nazi activities in 1934, he was forced to seek sanctuary in Nazi Germany. During his two year exile, he managed to advance to the position of deputy-editor for a national newspaper based in the city of Essen. He returned to Vienna following the Anschluss in March 1938, and a short time later was appointed editor of the national paper, German Telegraph. Equipped with such credentials, Kernmayer moved rapidly through Party ranks, and by 1939 was head of the Party Press Agency in Vienna. That advance was a precursor for a promotion that saw him made leader of the Press Dept. for the entire German Gau of Saarland / Lothringen in 1940. It was while serving as propaganda leader under Saarland Gauleiter, Josef Bürckel, that Kernmayer accumulated a wide range of contacts throughout the entire greater Reich. Details of Kernmayer's career suddenly became scarce following his voluntary induction into the Waffen SS division, *"Das Reich"* in 1941. Although there are no indications he faced any criminal charges for his war time activities, occupying forces did order a life-long ban on publishing as a consequence of his public statements during the war. Kernmayer would later circumvent the ban by simply writing under the pseudonym of Erich Kern.

Evidence of the political direction Kernmayer was espousing in 1946 was visible in his role in helping found the 'Gmundener Circle', a group of former leading SS and NSDAP members known for their energetic dispersal of neo-Nazi convictions. His pattern of involving himself in right-wing organizations would continue in 1948 with the Deutsche Reichs Party. Two years later, he helped establish the *"Help Network for former members of the Waffen SS"*, and in 1955, became involved with HIAG, an association set up to fight for the 'rights' of Waffen SS veterans. Despite these various activities, Kernmayer found time to write several revisionist books in which he described the war, 'as it really was'. In later years, his obstinate beliefs would find outlets through the NPD, a far right-wing political party in Germany, as well as his association with the publisher of the Deutsche National-Zeitung,

Gerhard Frey. Kernmayer would persist in spouting his versions of SS and Wehrmacht history right up until his death in 1991. Although many of these 'achievements' had yet to materialize in 1948, his reputation was such that Höttl did not hesitate having his valued compatriot join him in the newly established offices in Gmunden.

A second aspirant to Höttl's troupe was former SS Captain Karl Kowarik. In a profile that often mirrored Höttl's own chronicles, Kowarik's record of staunch anti-Communist leanings was traceable back to his experiences in the nationalistic German Gymnastic Association, and his father's membership in Georg von Schönerer's Greater German Party. Prior to joining the NSDAP in 1930, Kowarik was also involved in several right-wing organizations known to have promoted anti-semitic as well as anti-Communist propaganda. Once officially aligned with the Nazi Party, he rose to become the leader of the Hitler Youth for all of Austria within four years. Similar to many fellow Nazi brethren, Kowarik was arrested and jailed following the failed Dollfuss putsch in July 1934. Able to flee to Germany, he continued to administer the activities of the illegal Austrian Hitler Youth from exile, until the Anschluss in 1938 brought his immediate re-instatement to Vienna. Now a Captain in the SS, Kowarik gained further notoriety that year for his leading role in the activities surrounding *"Kristallnacht."* He was also reported to have participated in assorted criminal activities perpetrated by the Waffen SS during the latter stages of the war. Following the end of hostilities, he went on to become one of the founding members of the World Anti-Communist League,(WACL), an organization established by yet another purported CIC employee in the late 1940's.

Born December 20th, 1909 in Vienna, Wilhelm Landig was one of the first Austrians to publicly show support for the ascendant Adolf Hitler. As was the case with Kowarik and Kernmayer, Landig's involvement in the failed 1934 coup also forced him into exile in Germany, a banishment that directly led to his joining the SD and Waffen SS calvary division *"Florian Geyer"*. Posted to Berlin, he advanced to the rank of Staff Sergeant while working at the Worker Economic Institute. Authorized by Heinrich Himmler to join the throngs of Austrian Nazis streaming back to Vienna after the Anschluss, he worked on a number of top secret SD projects on Himmler's behalf, one of which reportedly delved into the occult.

Höttl:1999

"Himmler was captivated by such things as UFO's and aliens, things that you can't prove exist. He was strongly influenced by such people as clair-voyants, people who could see into the future. This fit into his whole make-up, such a believer of miracles. And of course for him, Hitler was someone who had been sent from God. A typical example,... when Mussolini was over-thrown in Rome, I went back there. My Italian connection and I quickly esta-blished where Mussolini was, ... As we reported that to Berlin, I saw what Himmler did. Although it was already known where he was, he wanted to find Mussolini. He took people out of the concentration camps, these clairvoyants, and those with pendulums, and put them up at Wannsee, which oddly enough was where the Wannsee Conference had been. They were well taken care of, could smoke and have alcohol, so they would have looked for Mussolini for years. It wasn't going well of course, so in their own way they tried to stretch out the time. Himmler came practically everyday and asked, 'Have you found him yet? Where is he?' and so on. I can attest to this because I witnessed it myself."

Beyond rummaging around in the supernatural, details of Landig's other wartime activities remained obscure. Wounded in the Balkans in 1944, he saw out his term of duty in relative safety, and after the war turned his attention to the cause of fighting Communism in his homeland. With his status already well known within the splintered National Socialist commu-nity, he soon became involved in right-wing organizations, helping to found the Europe Congress, an international association made up largely of for-mer SS officers. Before that was to happen however, he managed to find another pulpit for his beliefs as chairman of the neofascist organization, Austrian Socialist Movement (OSB). By mid-1948 Landig's political forum had expanded to include leadership of the European branch of the World Anti-Communist League (EUROWACL), as well as membership in the na-tionalistic Association of Independents, or VdU, a coterie that also served as the breeding ground for Karl Kowarik's early political career. The VdU would eventually mutate into the FPÖ, later a springboard for the aspira-tions of another right wing politician by the name of Jorg Haider.

Landig continued to promote his ideology through his own publishing house, Volkssturm-Landig-Publishing. Founded in 1961, with Karl Kowa-rik serving for a time as the business manager, it reportedly published material denying the Holocaust. Seven years after Kowarik's death in 1987, his son Helmut, himself a member of the Vienna regional council for the FPÖ, assumed control of the Volksturm Verlag and its catalogue, which included many of the anti-semitic works of his father and Landig. Linked in conviction as well as intention, Kernmayer, Kowarik and Landig represented the type of people the CIC was prepared to engage in its fight for 'democracy.'

Two other individuals to grace Höttl's initial roster were former Gau inspector for Upper Danube, Stefan Schachermayer, and Dr. Karl Ney, a Major in the Hungarian Military Intelligence Service, (HONVED). Born April 22nd 1912 in Wolfsbach, a small Austrian town between Steyr and Amstetten, Schachermayer joined the Austrian NSDAP in 1932. Appointed leader of the Party newspaper in 1936, he soon became a close confidant and aide to the Steiermark Gauleiter, August Eigruber. Although few details are known about Schachermayer's war time activities, he was at one point a member of the personnel at Schloss Hartheim, a Nazi euthanasia clinic in Austria, where future Treblinka extermination camp commandant, Franz Stangl and Belzec camp director Christian Wirth, oversaw the murders of thousands of *'disabled'* patients by gassing or lethal injections. Despite the implications of that association, and the fact a People's Court later sentenced Schachermayer to three years, Höttl met no objections when enlisting him into active service for his planned network.

Chosen to head the military sector of Höttl's network, Dr. Karl Ney was expected to assume responsibility for recruiting fellow Hungarians from Salzburg and Upper Austria for the planned *"stay behind"* networks, a task similar to one he had undertaken with Otto Skorzeny in 1944. Born November 8th, 1906, Ney first surfaced to public attention in 1939 as a member of a pro- German party in the Hungarian Parliament. A lawyer by profession, he traveled to Germany in 1942 to undergo several months of instruction at an SS training camp. Upon his return to Hungary, he helped establish the KABSZ, a paramilitary organization dedicated to fighting Communism. With the German occupation of Hungary in March 1944, Ney and the KAB-SZ acted as storm troopers for the newly installed Imredy government. Working in conjunction with Skorzeny, he and his troops also played a role in the October coup that brought Szalasi and the Arrow Cross Party to power. Shortly thereafter, Ney appears to have run afoul of the new leader, resulting in a demotion and loss of his Hungarian citizenship. Later that same year, his name appeared on a list of persons wanted in connection with the execution of several American prisoners captured behind enemy lines. In the last few months of the war, Ney led his brigade into many battles in Hungary and eastern Austria. Yet despite this notoriety, at war's end, Ney's alleged crimes somehow escaped the notice of occupying forces, an oversight that resulted in his even being selected to temporarily serve as the administrator of the former concentration sub-camp at Ebensee. Although he was removed from that position on suspicion of corruption in early 1946, neither that dismissal, nor rumours of other questionable activities, posed any threat to his inclusion into Höttl's growing entourage.

With his salient den of anti-Communists in place by mid-spring of 1948, Höttl was ready to re-instate his penchant for independence. Given that keeping Communists and their supporters under surveillance did not require excessive management, he was content to limit his visits to Gmunden headquarters to once a week. Administrative duties at CIC headquarters in Salzburg were deemed worthy of no more than a monthly appearance. Although some observers felt leaving his new associates to their own devices might make him vulnerable to betrayal, in reality there was little chance of that happening. Having clamoured to get aboard the CIC gravy train, few colleagues were about to risk dismissal by deceiving the man responsible for their inclusion. Although many of Höttl's associates would eventually use the opportunity to set their own priorities, in the beginning, gratitude and opportunism helped to fuse a superficial loyalty amongst participants. As far as concealing their endeavours from Austrian authorities was concerned, Höttl and his *people* did not have to be overly worried. As long as a steady stream of relevant information continued to flow in from the developing network of informants strewn across Austria, official criticism of how it was attained initially remained muted. As minor successes continued to mount however, it wasn't long before rumblings of apprehension began to make themselves apparent in certain quarters.

By the spring of '48, one and a half years had passed since Ernst Kaltenbrunner dropped from the gallows at Nuremberg. In the intervening period, variations on the whereabouts of his, and other treasures abandoned by various Nazi leaders had continued to flourish, fanned by sporadic discoveries made in the lakes and forests of Ausseerland. Long suspected of possessing intimate knowledge about secret locations, Höttl was repeatedly approached by parties interested in gaining details on the unaccounted for riches. For the most part, he was able to deflect such inquiries, but in April of 1948, he was caught off guard by the arrival of an unexpected visitor.

Elisabeth Kaltenbrunner's decision to travel to Alt Aussee that spring, was a direct result of the visit she had paid her husband shortly before his execution. Ostensibly arranged for the pair to share a last farewell, Frau Kaltenbrunner had managed to broach the issue of her future welfare and that of their children during their brief conversation. Both she and her husband knew such sessions were closely monitored by prison authorities, if for no other reason than to prevent a possible last minute suicide. As a result, the former RSHA leader had presumably exercised a degree of caution in his statements. Seeking to calm his distressed wife, he assured her that she needn't worry as *"Höttl knew what to do and would take care of everything"*. With his own sealed fate only hours away, Kaltenbrunner had little reason to lie, nor would implicating his old subordinate have been high on his limited agenda. The eleventh hour revelation was more likely a last ditch attempt to ease his conscience and provide for his family.

Relieved by the news or not, Frau Kaltenbrunner had no opportunity to verify her husband's pledge during Höttl's own lengthy detention. How she managed to support her family in the intervening years is not certain. In April '48 however, having learned Höttl was back in circulation, she concluded it time for a face to face meeting with the man she believed could see her husband's assurances honoured. In the months prior to her visit, she attempted to investigate Höttl's various peace missions to Switzerland, missions she felt, buttressed the claims made by her husband in 1946. Of particular interest was the story of secret Swiss accounts Höttl was alleged to have set up on behalf of the Gestapo. With no authentic record of her meeting with Höttl available, it is impossible to know precisely what was discussed during their encounter. Frau Kaltenbrunner's hasty departure shortly thereafter however, tends to suggest Höttl had merely claimed no knowledge of any promised arrangements.

Höttl: 1997

"I knew that Kaltenbrunner made deposits in an account in Switzerland, officially under his wife's name. When it was discovered, she had no knowledge of it and could also not make any use of it. She had many personal difficulties aside from the time when he was accused. Many personal things. This was a human tragedy."

Not long after Frau Kaltenbrunner had left Alt Aussee, a second unwelcome blip appeared on Höttl's radar. This time it came in the form of criminal proceedings initiated by the County Court in Linz. Charged with high treason for his membership in the illegal NSDAP between 1933 and 1938, Höttl was initially apprehensive. Previous American refusals to hand him over to Austrian authorities in Vienna could no longer be counted on as Linz lay in the western sector. As it happened, he needn't have worried. Still ill disposed to any impact a public trial of their protege might produce, the Americans reportedly used their influence to stonewall Linz prosecutors. Whether a consequence of that pressure, or simply the glacial pace of judicial bureaucracy, the Linz indictment would remain dormant until November, 1951, at which time all charges were dismissed as part of a general amnesty promoted by the German government.

Long before that was to occur, a third event was dropped into Höttl's path, this one involving the death of his father and subsequent American denial to let him attend the funeral in Vienna. Although Höttl knew that US policy towards making him accessible to Eastern authorities had not changed, he claimed to have deeply resented the American decision. It would be decades before he would finally admit the ruling had been a prudent one.

Höttl: 1999

"I couldn't go back to Vienna for my father's funeral because the list of people who were being sought was stored at the Enns border crossing, and I was on it. The Russian Secret Service was always especially dangerous. When they arrived in Vienna they read a number of the reports I had written that went to Berlin… they saw what an obvious enemy of Communism I was, and how dangerous I was for them because they could see that I knew a great deal.

We had worked a lot with Russians immigrants who had reported things and the Russian Secret Service had found these in Vienna. I was known by name as these reports were signed, they weren't anonymous, I had signed them Dr. Höttl, SS and so on. They were laying there and could be read at any time. They would have nabbed me right away. I would have landed in Siberia."

What Höttl failed to include in that belated disclosure was that at the time of their decision, the Americans had also been concerned over a recent spate of reports insinuating Höttl had initiated contact with known Soviet operatives, under the umbrella of his recruitment drive.

CIC informant *"Hermann"*: 1948

"Subject (Höttl) is currently engaged in forming an intelligence net which he plans to have in operation by the end of August 1948. Subject has contacted former German intelligence personnel who are now working as informants for all four occupying powers and has inquired of them if they will work for him. Subject is allegedly in contact with Ludwig Jedlicka, General Secretary of the Cominform for Austria, and Roman Gamottha, former police Commissioner in Vienna, and later head of the SD in Prague."

Despite inklings that Höttl was veering away from the anti-Communist guidelines, the Americans were reticent to directly accuse him of any breaches in protocol. Hoping to avoid de-railing plans for the network, they instead ordered Jedlicka and Gamottha (who would later became a leader of a Soviet intelligence network in East Germany), be placed under discreet observation. The agency's monitoring techniques however, were somewhat less than subtle, and shortly after the surveillance began, Höttl wrote to CIC headquarters demanding to know why his *'friend'* Jedlicka was being investigated by the CIC in Vienna. Although the differences were eventually ironed out, as a precaution, Höttl attempted to reduce CIC concerns by adopting a more diplomatic tone, carting out his patented explanation of needing to seek information 'from all sources'. Placated for the moment, CIC officials had no way of knowing that the incident was only the first of what would be many infractions to involve Eastern *'elements'*.

Although busy negotiating through the wave of unanticipated adventures in the spring of 1948, Höttl nevertheless continued preparations for his expanded network. By early July, Operation Montgomery, a program designed to gather intelligence and conduct espionage against Soviet forces in Hungary, was ready to activate. Parallel to that achievement however, a series of disturbing reports had been accumulating at CIC headquarters in Salzburg, reports which augmented the arguments of those who had been reluctant to hire Höttl in the first place. Suspecting Höttl had been exploring the possibility of marketing his wares beyond the CIC's realm, critics were able to use the reports to gain authorization for a limited surveillance. Höttl's espionage experience however, had taught him to be judicious and as a result, neither the surveillance nor a deeper analysis of the reports, yielded anything beyond innuendo. Seeking another venue to expose what they were convinced was Höttl's treachery, opponents decided to contact informants familiar with his recent activities. One of the first questioned by CIC officials was Adalbert Kungel, an employee of the Technical Information Branch (TIB) of the Allied European Command (EUCOM). The 37 year old Yugoslavian confirmed that Höttl had approached him, inquiring whether he would be interested in working for an intelligence network he claimed to be preparing. Kungel told interrogators he had chosen to decline the offer, convinced that Höttl was someone *"who, for money, would work for any and all nations"*. It was an assessment that would soon start emerging from other sources as well.

Fritz Fischer:
"I was fed up with the constant spying and reporting on people, and his practice of abandoning colleagues whenever he seemed that it might be dangerous for him. Höttl was a generous person when he wanted something, but if he couldn't get it, you became dispensable…He was a difficult person who liked to view himself as the 'grey eminence', always working in the background to achieve his own advantage."

Shortly after those comments on Höttl's unscrupulous pragmatism and apparent American willingness to tolerate it, Fischer broke off relations with his colleague and left Austria for a lucrative business offer in Germany.

On July 12th, 1948, it was the turn of thirty-seven year old Iris Scheidler to be questioned. A resident of Salzburg at the time she was brought before CIC investigators, the wife of Kaltenbrunner's former adjutant, and long-time friend of the Höttl family, described how she had come to learn of Höttl's frequent visits to the city over the previous two months. Claiming not to have been privy to the purposes of those visits, she told investigators she felt they had involved meetings with former German intelligence personnel, adding that despite his lack of visible employment, Höttl often acted as if he had a seemingly unlimited supply of money at his disposal.

News of Scheidler's candidness didn't take long to get back to Höttl. Realizing the lengths his CIC patrons were prepared to go in order to probe his activities, he decided it wise to make a tactical retreat. Momentarily shelving plans for discussions with other potential clients, he concentrated on completing work on a second planned network designed to infiltrate and monitor Communist organizations within Austria. Despite the progress made on *"Mount Vernon"* over the next few months, disquieting reports about Höttl's actions continued to land on the desk of CIC Major Edward Prix. Already responsible for translating and evaluating most of Höttl's intelligence submissions, Prix now found himself in the position of having to determine what percentage of Höttl's activities were in the best interests of the agency.

Throughout the score of testimonies, interviews, and musings Höttl delivered over the decades, seldom if ever, did he pause to ruminate on what life might have been like *"if only"*. One of the exceptions to that rule occurred in the mid 1990's, during an exchange with long time Bad Aussee resident and amateur historian, Michael Roithner. Roithner and Höttl were often seen sharing long walks around the lake at Alt Aussee, and it was during one such leisurely stroll that conversation turned to the theme of a *"life not lived"*. According to Roithner's recollections, Höttl had halted on the gravel pathway, taking time to reflect before mulling aloud that given another chance, he would have liked to become a university professor or gone into politics. Though the admission was not made with any strong sense of regret, Höttl must have sensed where the conversation might lead. Making it clear he had no intention of elaborating on his expressed preferences, he changed the subject and resumed his unhurried gait.

Any opportunity Höttl might have had to pursue politics directly had been cast aside in the early '30's, and another twenty years would pass before a chance to probe prospects surfaced again. Between those two junctures however, the political landscape in Austria changed dramatically. Since the end of the war, the country had been divided into four separate zones, each occupied by one of the Allied victors. Despite conflicting ideologies, the four administering powers, the US, USSR, France and Great Britain had agreed to institute procedures to form a national government of representatives. In line with that goal, a grand coalition was elected on November 25th, 1945, comprised of the Austrian People's Party (ÖVP) and Austrian Socialist Party (SPÖ). Despite their purported mandate, the new government with Leopold Figl (ÖVP) as Chancellor, could not affect major change without the approval of the occupying powers. As cumbersome as this mechanism was, it did manage to function. Four years later, national elections were announced as part of an overall plan to return Austria to full sovereignty. In order to allow parties time to organize and campaign, the date set for elections was October 9th, 1949. According to a survey taken earlier that year, analysts forecast the vote would be split evenly between the ÖVP on the right and the SPÖ on the left, leaving the outcome in the hands of 500,000 voters being allowed to exercise their franchise for the first time since the end of the war. Aside from those who had come of age in the previous four years, a large portion of the new voting block was made up of former Nazis, whose voting rights had been withdrawn in 1945 as part of Austria's limited de-nazification program. Even before the election had been officially announced, the established parties began to devote themselves to attracting this potential mass of *"new"* votes. According to Höttl, one of the first political figures to promote contact with the former Nazis was Josef Krainer, an ÖVP politician and head of the State government of the Steiermark. The man actually assigned to explore the possibility of cooperation on behalf of the ÖVP, was Julius Raab.

Born in St. Polten on November 29th, 1891, Raab was no newcomer to Austrian politics. Reportedly included as a potential Minister in the ill- fated Kaltenbrunner government proposed to the Americans in April 1945, he had later been one of the founding members of the Austrian People's Party (ÖVP). A rising star in the party, he would later be elected Chancellor, serving as head of the Austrian Government from 1953 to 1961. Several years before that pinnacle would be reached, Raab had concentrated his political expertise on how the ÖVP might succeed in gaining power in the 1949 election. To help procure the Nazi vote, he reportedly acquired the services of ex-Nazi journalist, Dr. Manfred Jasser. Jasser was assigned the task of convincing the financially strapped Party of Independents (VdU), their cause would be better served under the aegis of the ÖVP. To help achieve that goal, he was allegedly given the sum of 600,000 Austrian shillings, and the promised assistance of Dr. Wilhelm Höttl. Höttl later claimed he had been drawn into ÖVP machinations as a result of an introduction to Raab, arranged by his old friend and colleague, Professor Dr. Taras Borodajkewycz. The old professor had sought to bring about a reconciliation between the former Nazis and the Roman Catholic based parties ever since being banned from resuming his teaching post at the University following the Nazi defeat. Despite that post-war jolt to his career, Borodajkewycz had chosen to remain in Vienna, accepting part-time work for Soviet officials, combing the stacks at the Vienna State Archives for material that might prove of interest to them. According to sources, many of his off-hours were spent cultivating contacts within the ÖVP, encouraging party leaders to reach an understanding with the ex-Nazis, to increase their chances of winning the long anticipated election. As a result of furtive discussions held in the spring of 1949, plans were made for a secret meeting to be held at the Villa Thonet in Oberweis, a small town not far from the CIC office in Gmunden.

On May 28th, Raab and other ÖVP leaders sat down with representatives of the former Nazis, to discuss ways of fusing their respective voting blocs. In addition to Raab and Jasser, attending the meeting on behalf of the ÖVP were Upper Austria party leader, Dr. Albert Schöpf, National delegate for Steiermark, Herr Karl Brunner, and President of the National Council, Dr. Alfred Maletta. Acting as spokesmen for the Nazis were former Vienna Hitler Youth leader, Walter Pollak, well-known NS lawyer, Dr. Erich Führer, and delegates from Linz, Graz and Braunau. Also believed present was Theo Wührer, a former SS journalist and adjutant to Ernst Kaltenbrunner. Rounding out the list was Borodajkewycz himself, who reportedly came with a list of Nazi demands. In return for delivering their bloc of votes to the ÖVP, the ex-Nazis expected to receive 25 seats in the national legislature, several people named to coveted posts, and the replacement of Justice Minister, Dr. Josef Gero (VdU) with Dr. Egbert Mannlicher, a former department head in the Justice Ministry. According to Höttl, Gero's removal was demanded because of his having been a driving force behind the country's de-Nazification laws. Completing the list was the request that a mutual candidate be selected to run for the federal Presidency.

Höttl's own role at the Oberweis summit can best be described as murky. In later years, he would claim his involvement had been part of the general CIC assignment to monitor groups and report on their activities. While that may have been partially true, a much more plausible scenario was that he had hoped to gain a foothold in the future political landscape. As it was, others involved in the secret negotiations held disparate views towards Höttl's input. While some former Nazis considered him one of their own, members of the ÖVP contingent tended to view him as little more than a hovering opportunist, tolerated solely because his links to the Americans could possibly serve as a buffer between themselves and inquisitive Austrian authorities.

Whatever Höttl's true function or goal, the dream of merging the two sides was derailed when news of the sequestered meeting became public. Convinced they had uncovered a neo-Nazi conspiracy, the Austrian State police proceeded to arrest several of the ex-Nazis who had attended the meeting. Following the implosion of the amalgamation plans, an atmosphere of last minute pragmatism quickly emerged amongst the political parties. Although having openly displayed its Nazi leanings, the VdU went on to accept financial backing from the SPÖ, which hoped a stabilized VdU would siphon votes away from their main opponent, the ÖVP. The *"formers"*, as the ex-Nazis were referred to, decided to run under the banner of the Independent Voters Association or WdU. On election day, they managed to garner 489,273 votes, a figure that translated into 16 seats in the Upper House. The number was telling. In May 1945, Austria's population had stood at seven million, 540,000 of whom had been registered members of the Nazi Party, a higher per capita membership than even Germany itself. Four and a half years later, nearly half a million voters chose to cast their ballot for the WdU, a clear signal of how few had altered their idealogical outlook despite the de-nazification program between 1946 – 1947.

Despite the fallout from the Oberweis escapade, the ÖVP recovered to form the new government. As with most newly elected bodies, it was generous in rewarding its various supporters, with teaching posts, directorships and economic positions among the prizes awarded. Borodajkewycz was appointed to the World Trade School, Dr. Hermann Raschhofer a right-wing historian received a professorship, and Dr. Manfred Jasser, made director of an Austrian publishing house. Others did not fare as well. Once in power, ÖVP officials made it clear *"the likes of Höttl"* were not welcome and his services no longer required, which helps explain why shortly after the election, Höttl switched his allegiance to the VdU. Although his desire for political influence had suffered a clear setback, Höttl feigned ambivalence towards the ÖVP's rejection, denying he had ever entertained overt political ambitions, claiming he had found a fulfilling outlet for his beliefs within the *"Gmundener Circle"*.

CIC File:
"... an uncouth and characterless individual, whose reports are over-inflated and a mixture of overt and semi-overt information."

By the late spring of 1949, denunciatory memos highlighting Höttl's shortcomings were surfacing with disturbing frequency. Although somewhat pre-occupied by the political manoeuvrings underway since the election announcement, Höttl still managed to stave off those handlers at CIC headquarters calling for his head. As critics sensed a direct attack on his person was getting them nowhere, they attempted to build momentum amongst wavering officials by pushing for an internal probe and impartial assessment of the material Mount Vernon was producing.

CIC File:
"... a low calibre of information, sloppy and contradictory, often drawn from garbled newspaper reports or completely fabricated."

The Montgomery network was also included in the investigation, and did not fare much better, criticized as having supplied only general information or false reports. Strangely enough, Höttl was not overly perturbed by the turning tide. Rather than instituting changes in the pace or quality of his submissions, he proceeded to seek and cultivate additional contacts, something that did not go unnoticed by his CIC patrons.

CIC file:
"... a very active, tenacious and ruthless person, shrewd, versatile, and very ambitious, dubious character,... who keeps up a large correspondence with persons involved in intelligence activities, who could be of use to him in the future."

By mid-summer matters had reached a critical stage. Furnished with evidence of dubious contacts and shoddy material, on August 9th, CIC officials recommended both Vernon and Montgomery be mothballed. Höttl however, remained on the company payroll for another three months. Finally summoned to CIC offices in Linz on Dec. 1st., Alpberg, alias Willi

Goldberg, alias Wilhelm Goldberg, alias Dr. Ostermann, alias Dr. Willi Holten, was officially informed by CIC handlers that his services were no longer required. Höttl had not been oblivious to the possibility of dismissal, or the implications it could have on his credibility within other intelligence circles. In the days and weeks leading up to his actual ousting, he actively spread word of his dissatisfaction with current arrangements, telling anyone who would listen he was miffed at having been told to reduce his expenditures and account for every dollar dispensed to him. He also went out of his way to allude he would soon no longer be bound by these rules of engagement. As a result of those concerted efforts, by the time announcement of his exit did arrive, it was not terribly difficult to make it appear he had resigned his post in protest.

One of the reasons the American had taken so long to act, despite evidence Höttl had been duping them for months, was the unforeseen risk of setting a disgruntled, knowledgable operative loose on a market rife with potential buyers. Their delay was also prolonged by the fact a number of officials were not willing to lose face and admit they were being fed bogus information. Combined with the inherent secrecy and hubris within the intelligence community's hierarchy, circumstances simply did not lend themselves for the rapid and easy removal of an acknowledged dud.

Fritz Fischer: 1999

"The Americans, slowly came to view Höttl as the enemy. They only supported him to insure that he didn't go over to the other side with his knowledge and experience. "

Fritz Fischer: 1999
"He was always prepared for the next step while still engaged in perfor-
ming the present one. He was someone who wouldn't undertake anything wi-
thout at least three or four separate assurances or alternatives behind him... "

Thanks to the months of American dawdling, Höttl had plenty of time
to assess a number of other venues. As a result, the thirty-four year old husband and father of three was ready to pirouette on to the open market even
before his CIC bonds had been dissolved. What Höttl didn't know but may
have suspected, was that in spite of having been officially removed from
active CIC service, elements within the American intelligence community
continued to monitor their former protege, convinced that cutting him loose entirely would be at their own peril.

Well aware he was living on borrowed time with the CIC, Höttl had
been on the lookout for a front that could camouflage plans to offer his
wares to new and competing patrons. The opportunity came shortly after
his dismissal in December, when he opted to purchase a small publishing
house in Linz. Not only did the business have the advantage of being located near many of the contacts developed to date, it also offered the potential of alleviating his long simmering literary aspirations. Once the decision to procure the Nibelungen Publishing House had been made, the next
hurdle was to secure the necessary financing. Höttl would later claim the
80,000 Schilling needed came from saved portions of his CIC salary. Such
a feat may not have been as implausible as it sounded. The CIC post-war
apparatus in Austria had been funded to the tune of $1-$2 million a year,
with an overall staff of around 1000 men. CIC files confirm Höttl had
received several thousand dollars a month during his two year tenure.
Considering his acknowledged reluctance to obey 'petty regulations' regarding his financial management, many suspected that portions of the
money intended for informants, had been secretly funnelled back into his
own account. An article in a 1996 issue of the Austrian magazine, *'Profil'*
alluded to certain *'mislaid'* CIC payments, claiming Höttl had been able to
accrue a sum between 100,000 and 120,000 Schillings, by combining missing funds with income derived from selling information to other intelligence clients.

Over the years, other arcane theories would arise as to how the purchase had been funded, including one that implied the CIC itself had played a direct role. Given the American intelligence community's tendency for getting involved in odd ventures, as well as their urge to keep an eye on Höttl, such a scenario cannot be entirely ruled out. An article in a German magazine in 1953, claimed Nibelungen's funding came from 150,000 Schillings Höttl had raised through the sale of jewelry reportedly given to him by his old friend, Fritz Westen. Citing the Casa Picolo Cafe in Vienna as the location where the alleged transaction took place, it pointed to a certain Dr. Otto Schott as the actual executor of the sale. Schott, was later appointed executive assistant at the Nibelungen Publishing House.

No matter how the issue funding was resolved, Höttl still faced the problem of an Austrian law which prohibited convicted Nazis from owning a company. That mild irritation was overcome by simply selecting his wife, Elfriede, to serve as owner and figurehead director. Although she lacked experience, had three children at home to contend with, and patently had no intention of running the firm, Austrian officials did not hesitate to authorize the sale. Elfriede's meagre credentials were also of no concern to her husband, who had already taken the liberty of hiring Dr. Emil van Tongel to oversee the day to day operations of NPH. Van Tongel's qualifications for the post were considerable. Born in Leitmeritz an der Elbe, on October 27th, 1902, he had obtained a degree in law before abruptly deciding to become a pharmacist. Much like Höttl, van Tongel was drawn to the NSDAP at an early age, officially joining in 1932. His long association with the Party led to work with a number of illegal NSDAP papers in Austria, before being offered a position at the German Propaganda Ministry in Vienna. Reported to have remained an ardent Nazi long after the war, van Tongel would go on to serve on the National Council of the FPÖ. With such a 'trusted' associate to perform the bulk of the daily tasks at NPH, Höttl was free to turn his attention to the revered goal of writing his own recollection of recent history.

Höttl 1956:

"As a responsible historian, I maintain to this day that 'Die geheime Front'
(The Secret Front) is historically sound as far as all the essentials are concerned.
It was of course necessary to add minor literary embellishments, since that is
the only way to sell enough copies, purely historical works not being known as
commercial successes. Just at the time when this book was published I had to
depend on it for my income."

The genesis for Höttl's first memoir is thought to have taken root during
his time at Nuremberg. Although progress on the project was limited by the
strict prison regime, he did manage to keep a log of his various encounters
with top-ranking Nazis, hoping to one day include the material in his envisioned opus. In the first six months after his release in late 1947, familial duties
and CIC activities further delayed advances, but by the summer of 1948,
enough material had been assembled to begin exploratory talks with publishers. Lacking a completed manuscript, he initially made due with a two and a
half page synopsis, in which the book was described as an historical characte-
rization of the German Intelligence Service from 1933 to 1945, written by a
figure, who *"had been in a position to know what was going on"*. The figure in
question was Walter Hagen, the pseudonym Höttl selected to avoid being
lumped together with other Nazis, whose works he dismissed as being rooted
in sensationalism.

Having set the bar for historical accuracy high enough to foster interest
in the unfinished book, Höttl deftly backtracked, telling publishers his ability
to back up certain statements with documented evidence had been damaged
by Hitler's order to destroy all the intelligence files shortly before the German
collapse. In spite of that handicap, he promised his prospective partners that
proof of the book's authenticity could either be extracted from various eye-wit-
nesses still alive, or the vault of confiscated documents now in the hands of
the Allied victors. Despite such a blatant exculpation, the outline continued to
elicit favourable responses, as evidenced by a series of letters Höttl exchanged
with an *"old acquaintance"* in the fall of 1948. Seeking the expertise of a qualified literary agent, he wrote to a man named Kurt Ponger, proudly announcing that publishers in both Austria and Switzerland had responded positi-
vely, and that there had even been inquiries from Time-Life in America.

Höttl: 1953

"During my stay at Nuremberg, where I was a witness and confined in the court building, I became acquainted with Ponger. This was in the year 1946. At that time Ponger was active with the prosecution in the trial against members of the SS Economic and Administrative Office. At this time he had nothing to do with me since I was a witness in the trial against major war criminals, as well as in the so called Wilhelmstrasse Trial. Ponger, was frequently in my vicinity during interrogations as was not uncommon in Nuremberg. He made a pleasant impression on me at the that time since he always handled himself in a humane and thoroughly courteous manner in contrast to many other of the interrogators."

Höttl: 1999

"I had business dealings with him (Ponger), in connection with publishing. I wanted to bring my book out and had worked with publishing houses, and Ponger had good connections with the press. Before a book is released, it is mentioned in the press, and Ponger handled that for me."

Born in Vienna on July 29th, 1913, Kurt L. Ponger's early life in the capital appears to have gone largely undocumented until the early 1930's, when he and another Viennese native by the name of Otto Verber, eight years his junior, joined the Austrian Communist Youth Movement. Branded as one of the loudest critics against *"clerical Fascism"*, Ponger gained a degree of notoriety from taking part in several street demonstrations against the policies of both Chancellors Dollfuss and Schüssnigg. Already recognized as Communist sympathizers, following the Anschluss in '38, both Ponger and Verber faced the additional threat of Nazi persecution because of their Jewish heritage. Convinced conditions were not going to improve any time soon, Verber and his family left Vienna for New York City. Verber's older sister, Vera, whom Ponger had been courting at the time, chose to flee to England. Shortly after her departure, Ponger had been detained by Austrian police and sent to the Dachau concentration camp. Interned at Dachau until his transfer to the Buchenwald KZ in September, he was released in March 1939 on the condition he leave the Reich, and refrain from divulging details of his imprisonment. Managing to obtain a British passport, Ponger made his way to England to reunite with Vera. While in London, the pair joined the English Communist Party and became involved with an organization set up to assist Austrian exiles. In February 1940, they left for New York City, settling into an apartment at 773 Columbia Ave. not far from where Otto Verber was residing with his new Austrian wife, Eva Beer.

With the full force of Cold War paranoia still a few years distant, being a registered Communist in the US in 1940 did not yet hold the same stigma as it would. Membership in the American Communist Party (ACP) in fact, remained legal right up until 1950. Taking advantage of their political freedom, the Pongers and Verbers all became affiliated with the American Communist Party in 1942, joining the same New York branch that had included Julius and Ethel Rosenberg as members. That involvement with the ACP, would later fuel rumours that Ponger and Verber had *"gone over"* to the Soviets as early as 1933.

While in New York, the pair divided their time between studies at New York University, and activities with two Austro-American student groups, later suspected as fronts for assisting Communist spies infiltrate the US. After the US entry into WWII in 1941, both men decided to sign up with the American Armed Forces. Despite their apparent predilection for Communism, neither encountered any barriers enlisting, and in mid 1942 were sent for training at various US facilities. Once courses at the Military Intelligence Training School at Camp Ritchie, Maryland were completed, both were officially integrated into the US Army intelligence corps and sent overseas. Because of his fluency in French, Verber was assigned to work as a liaison officer with the French Army. Ponger on the other hand, was earmarked for interrogation work, interviewing and translating for German prisoners of war.

Following their discharge from the Army at the end of the war, the pair returned to the US. Having become naturalized Americans in the interim, both were offered civilian assignments and returned to Germany to work as translators/ interrogators with the Office of the Chief Counsel of the International Military Tribunal, in preparation for the upcoming trials in Nuremberg. Given that Ponger and Höttl both had extensive backgrounds in the intelligence field, and found themselves in an environment conducive to absorbing an inordinate amount of privileged information, there were certainly grounds for their being drawn to each other. Although Höttl claimed their relationship at Nuremberg had been little more than passing, records show there was ample opportunity for them to have conducted regular communication. According to the directory of Military Tribunal personnel stationed in Nuremberg at the time, Ponger was listed as a civilian emplo-yee, residing at Novallisstr. 14. As a result of his successful application to switch residences in the fall of 1945, Höttl's new accommodation was loca-ted at Novallisstr. 24.

Once having accomplished its primary goal of prosecuting top Nazi leaders, the main court of the International Military Tribunal formally adjourned in October 1946. Although their assignments were officially over, Ponger and Verber were requested to stay on in Nuremberg, ostensibly to assist in the series of lower-level trials scheduled to follow. As part of his new duties, which included de-briefing soldiers returning from prisoner of war camps, and interviewing individuals recently escaped from behind the Iron Curtain, Ponger was occasionally required to travel to Vienna. Whether of his own making or one presented by his superiors, it was while in Vienna that the idea of establishing a more permanent base there was hatched. Ponger would later claim the concept had simply been a means of creating a second career for himself, once his official tour of duty ended. Other evidence however, indicated the plan was carried out with the full backing of American intelligence officials, intent on setting up a reliable front from which to carry out intelligence activities. Considering the thicket of intrigue post-war Vienna had become, it was for all intensive purposes, a bit of both.

One of the first steps towards establishing the Vienna base actually took place in a New York courtroom. Although the application for incorporation had been made several months earlier, on October 25th, 1946, a US judge formally announced the Central European Press and Literary Agency (CEPLA) into existence. Making up the board of directors at the new company, whose offices were located at 100 42nd St. NYC., but whose letterhead boasted branch offices in Vienna and Zurich, were Kurt and Vera Ponger, George Mandel, and Peter Brody, with Vera Ponger named as nominal director. Immediately after its incorporation, the company began to issue stocks in order to raise capital. Although that was nothing out of the ordinary for a new company, records show that over the next four years less than 25 shares would be sold, with the majority of those purchased by the directors of the company themselves. Suspicions the fledgling company had been getting external support were increased when corporate tax records from 1946 to 1953 revealed it to have earned no taxable income for each of its seven years in business. The theory that CEPLA had been a CIC front from the start, was strengthened by the fact that less than a year after its inception, Ponger applied to its board for permission to act as the company's official European representative in Vienna. Granted a mandate to tackle the company's purported rapid expansion in the East, for the next fifteen months, Ponger juggled his time between continuing duties in Nuremberg and his new commitments in Vienna. When official duties with the Military Tribunals came to an end in October 1948, within days, both Ponger and Verber had packed up their families and re-located permanently to Vienna.

Much like its German counterpart, in 1948 Vienna was still a divided city, split into four sectors by the occupying powers, France, the US, the Soviet Union, and Britain. Considering their new citizenship, and the country they had sworn allegiance to, one might have expected both families to have moved into the American sector. Ponger and his wife however, requested and received permission to take up residence in the Soviet sector, moving with their one year old daughter, Elizabeth, into a relatively luxurious four room apartment at Paulanerstr. 7 in Vienna's 4th district. Despite working for a company whose records indicated limited success, Ponger reportedly had the means to employ two maids, a photo assistant, and a nanny in his new milieu. In addition to those expenditures, he also found the resources to hire a former AGFA engineer from West Germany to construct an elaborate photo facility in the apartment. Outfitted with a car with US plates, he was able to make the short journey to the CEPLA office on Schönbrunnerstr. 47 in the 5th district with relative ease.

Otto and Eva Verber managed to find accommodations in the American sector, moving in at Wilhelm-Busch Gasse 32 in Vienna's 19th district. Now also on the CEPLA payroll, Verber spent most of his time at the office in Vienna. Ponger on the other hand, reportedly used his position to mingle in the various cultural and literary salons of Europe, building up a sizeable and impressive list of contacts on both sides of the Iron Curtain, despite the stringent travel restrictions in effect at the time.

◆

Höttl's letter to Ponger in the fall of '48, was indicative of the style their correspondence would assume over the next few years. Vague to the point of being obscure, it offered a brief outline of the book and mention of Höttl's own literary contacts, yet fell short of formally requesting Ponger's aid in securing a publisher. Ponger nevertheless seems to have taken it upon himself to use his connections to explore the book's viability.

Within six months he was able to inform Höttl that prospects were 'looking good', but that interested parties had made further cooperation dependant on receipt of a completed manuscript. Although it would have been a simple matter to inform interested publishers the book was still a *"work in progress"*, a concept most would have accepted, Höttl refused to agree to any sort of deadline. In a move that was both confrontational, as well as of little apparent benefit, he added a new element to potential negotiations, by announcing he had no intention of providing a final copy unless the publisher agreed to simultaneously accept the memoirs of his old colleague, Edmund Glaise-Horstenau. What prompted Höttl to tie the potential success of his own book to that of his old colleague remains uncertain. Whatever the reason, by late summer '49, the stipulation was quietly abandoned.

In spite of the continuing absence of a completed manuscript, Ponger did remarkably well in maintaining publishers' interest. Hoping to coax Höttl to submit at least portions of what he believed was the nearly completed book, he dangled the prospect of having 'The Secret Front' serialized in an American publication. After initially expressing interest, Höttl backed away from the offer, telling Ponger that for the time being, he would have to continue placating publishers with the synopsis. Considering the awkward situation Höttl's stubbornness placed him in, there was reason to believe Ponger's loyalty and persistence may have been due to other factors. Some observers would later speculate the whole 'book saga' had been nothing more than a facade to justify continued contact between the two men, contact that was suspected to have revolved around the exchange of intelligence.

The likelihood the book had been part of Höttl's dual track strategy was strengthened by the fact he had been carrying on his own search for a publisher, one that also included negotiations for serialization. But in spite of all the intrigue and delays, the book was ready for publication by the beginning of 1950. Rather than working with Ponger however, Höttl abruptly announced *"Die geheime Front"* was to make its debut through the auspices of his own Nibelungen Publishing House. Despite what was viewed as a repudiation of the legwork he had conducted on Höttl's behalf, Ponger showed no signs of having been slighted, further fuelling speculation their relationship had exceeded the boundaries of mere artistic endeavours.

With the issue of a publisher now resolved, there was still the obstacle of the so called *"Verbot"* law to be overcome. Enacted in 1947, the law was designed to prohibit *'incorrigible'* Nazis from spreading propaganda through the publication of their writings. On January 24th, 1950, Höttl wrote to the Austrian Federal President in Vienna, requesting exemption from Articles 3 and 4 of the statute. Judging from the lack of response in government circles, his attempt to portray the book as history seen through the eyes of a faithful and patriotic Austrian, seems to have fallen wide of the mark. For some reason however, the law did not apply to serialization. Two days before his letter to the President, 'Die geheime Front' had made its debut in the Austrian paper, *"Die Press"*. Regular instalments appeared for the next fifteen weeks, before concluding on April 22nd. Publication of the book itself took place later that year, even though Höttl would not receive official exemption until November 1951.

Much like the memoirs of Walter Schellenberg and Otto Skorzeny which went on to earn *"small fortunes"* on the international market, Höttl's work was slated for success, reportedly selling over 20,000 copies in Austria alone. With a contract that called for 9% for the first 5000 exemplars and 10% thereafter, the royalties, combined with those obtained from publication of the English version a year later, were enough to finance the construction of a family home in Alt Aussee, as well as the purchase of an apartment for his mother. The only thing to temporarily mar Höttl's success in attaining a slice of immortality, was an allegation that surfaced shortly after the book's release.

Rather than issuing an outright denial to the accusation it had not come from his own hand, Höttl simply rejected what he claimed were insinuations against his *"artistic integrity"*. Amazingly enough, the strategy worked and not long after the rumours abated, publishers ordered editions in several other languages. It would take decades before Höttl was finally prepared to admit an old friend had indeed been involved in the creation of the book. The man long suspected as Höttl's ghost writer was the journalist Dr. Anthony (Toni) Böhm, a colleague from Vienna days, who with Höttl's assistance, had risen to become the Balkan Referat in the Information Dept. of the Foreign Office during the war. Clearly designed to take the wind out of his critics' sails, albeit belatedly, Höttl confessed Böhm had been paid a monthly salary for his assistance, but insisted his role in the book's development had been much smaller than opponents claimed.

Rumours of of a ghost writer however, had not been the only repercussion to Höttl's literary success. Incensed over the attention the serialization was showering on him, Austrian authorities still eager to hold him accountable for his past, initiated legal proceedings on February 2nd, 1950, again charging him with membership in the SS during the illegal days of the Austrian NSDAP. No longer under the protective wing of the CIC, Höttl nevertheless managed to slip through the net laid by Linz prosecutors by merely supplying false information about his true date of entry into the SD. Able to back up his claim with the support of several *witnesses*, the case was dismissed before ever coming to trial.

Given the fierce competition that existed between various intelligence services in post-war Europe, even amongst those ostensibly on the same side, it was not difficult for freelance hustlers to gain a footing within several rival agencies. One of the first groups Höttl chose to approach after his dismissal from the CIC, was the Gehlen Organization (OG), the German intelligence service founded and supported by the Americans, and led by former Nazi General Reinhard Gehlen.

American preoccupation with General Reinhard Gehlen (1902 – 1979) stemmed from his days as the top Soviet expert in German Army Intelligence. From 1942 until the close of the war, Gehlen had reportedly accumulated a massive amount of information on the USSR, allegedly often attained by the blackmail and torture of captured Soviet POW's. In March 1945, as their future was about to be drastically altered, he and several of his senior officers microfilmed their vast stock of files on the USSR, and had it buried on an Alm in the Austrian Alps. Following his surrender to American troops in May, Gehlen was initially pegged as 'just another Nazi' and interned at the Glasenbach camp near Salzburg. While at Glasenbach, he chose to reveal his true identity, along with the existence of the hidden microfilm. The revelation had its desired effect and within days he was being personally de-briefed by several high ranking US Army officers, amongst them, General Edwin L. Sibert and Gen. Walter Bedell Smith, chief of staff to the European Supreme Commander, Gen. Dwight D. Eisenhower. Astonished and disturbed by Gehlen's expansive knowledge and predictions of Soviet intentions in post-war Europe, Smith, who would later serve as both US Ambassador to Moscow and Director of the CIA, quickly agreed to negotiate a deal. Descriptions vary as to what happened next. One version pictured Gehlen being hustled aboard Eisenhower's private plane and flown to the US, despite an Allied agreement from the Yalta summit, that demanded all German officers involved in *"Eastern area activities"* be turned over to Soviet authorities. A second version claimed that before agreeing to cooperate, the 43 year old Nazi successfully bartered for his own release as well as that of several staff members. Plans were being made for Gehlen to set up shop at US Army headquarters in Wiesbaden, when shots were fired at his car, prompting the decision to transfer him immediately to Fort Hunt, Virginia. Once in the States, he was subjected to another series of de-briefings, this time with such US officials as Army General George V. Strong and OSS mandarin, Allen Dulles. A deal was eventually hammered out, calling for American support in establishing an intelligence network within Germany, in exchange for the guarantee of a continuous flow of information on the Russians. Armed with the promise of American assistance, purported to have ultimately reached the sum of $200 million, Gehlen was returned to Germany in 1946, to begin operations in the town of Pullach, just south of Munich. Initially placed under the control of the US Army, management of the fledgling organization was eventually passed to the jurisdiction of the CIA. In April, 1956, with the blessing of both the American and German governments, OG evolved into West Germany's official foreign intelligence agency, the Deutsche Bundesnachrichtendienst or BND. During his tenure with OG, and later as head of the BND, Gehlen had an enormous impact on American policy and decision making. So profound was that influence, that decades later an official of the International War Group, responsible for vetting top secret files for eventual release, summed up American support for him as having been nothing less than *"a horrendous mistake, morally, politically and in pragmatic intelligence terms"*. (Richard Breilman)

Höttl had contributed to that mistake, albeit in a minor fashion, through his association with a man named Baron Heinrich von Mast. Born in the Sudetenland on August 26th, 1887, Mast, often known only as 'Harry', had seen service with German Army Intelligence (Abwehr) in Munich, before being transferred to Linz in the mid 1930's. Arrested and jailed by the Austrians as a suspected spy, he remained in custody until the Anschluss in March 1938, at which time he returned to Linz in the role of a military security officer. Recruited by the CIC after the war, Mast was drawn into the services of the Gehlen Organization in mid-1947, and made station chief for Linz by the end of the year. Although Höttl had intermittent dealings with Mast during his own CIC tenure in Gmunden, it wasn't until his dismissal and the launch of Nibelungen (NPH), that their level of contact became more frequent. A portion of their increased contact reportedly revolved around a proposal Mast had presented to OG officials, calling for NPH to be used as a front to acquire material from Höttl's discontinued network of agents. According to Mast's plan, secret intelligence dispatches destined for OG, were to be concealed amidst NPH's general correspondence and smuggled across the border. Whatever concerns OG may have had about the proposed venture, Höttl's tarnished reputation with the CIC was apparently not one of them.

Once the plan was approved, couriers recruited by Mast and NPH's deputy director, Dr. Otto Schott, began to transport the latest Austrian and Balkan intelligence data from Linz to Munich. An example of how the operation functioned was evident from an assignment carried out by a man by the name of Rudiger Lippmann. Born in 1929, in Buanaberg, Czechoslovakia, Lippmann moved to Bad Reichenhall, on the German-Austrian border shortly after the war. In 1947 he began attending classes at the Commercial Academy in Salzburg. As the studies required frequent travel between the two countries, Lippmann was an ideal candidate for Höttl's fledgling 'news service'. How and when he was recruited is not clear, but once on board, Lippmann soon began conveying documents across the border, using his student status as a cover. According to sources, NPH 'correspondence' was sent to an address in Salzburg twice a month. Lippmann's task was to retrieve the material and assure it was safely smuggled across the Austrian frontier, before being forwarded to specified recipients within Germany. In later testimony, Lippmann claimed not to have known the contents of the documents he was funnelling to Germany, nor any of the recipients. One letter however, had been of particular interest to him, largely because he came to meet its recipient shortly after posting it to an address in Munich. In subsequent conversations with Elisabeth Franke, Lippmann learned she had been a secretary to Höttl's Amt VI colleague, Wilhelm Waneck, during the war. According to Lippmann, Franke informed him the material being shunted back and forth across the border was simply research information for a book Höttl was writing. Why such elaborate methods were needed for the exchange of simple research material was left unanswered.

Whether Lippmann or others were aware of it at the time or not, his numerous journeys were being monitored by the CIC. Through the surveillance, officials determined that on return trips, Lippmann often carried West German assignments destined for various agents in the East, confirming their suspicions that Höttl was using people and facilities from his earlier networks. The monitoring also established that certain couriers were involved in smuggling illegal goods to the lucrative black market in Munich. Aware that a healthy portion of the smuggled information was ending up at OG, CIC concerns over Höttl's participation in the operation were initially muted by the fact a number of people within the Gehlen Organization still deemed the intelligence of significant value. Nonetheless, as a precaution, CIC officials sent a series of memos to their OG colleagues, warning that a considerable number of Höttl's previous reports had been graded as *"worthless, inflated or possibly fabricated"*, and voicing their suspicions he was 'involved in extensive intelligence activities with almost anyone willing to purchase his findings'. Such counsel should have prompted an immediate investigation, but with the growing tensions of the Cold War placing increasing pressure on competing agencies, Höttl and his cohorts were able to continue catering to the frantic demand for *'reliable'* intelligence, however flawed the material may have been.

In spite of the functioning partnership developed with OG, which presumably produced sufficient compensation, Höttl was bent on expanding his list of clientele. To assist in that task, he once again turned to Baron 'Harry' Mast. Over the ensuing months Mast would guide numerous prospective patrons in Höttl's direction, convincing many western operatives he had also been working for the Military Intelligence sector (MIS) of Soviet Intelligence. But as with many dubious agents at the time, rather than damaging their credibility and limiting access to new 'customers', such innuendo often promoted co-operation with other agencies, which believed the suspected treachery could be manipulated and used to their benefit.

One successful overture credited to Mast's account, involved the French Intelligence Service, known as the *"Deuxième Bureau"*. *"Zugang"* to the DB reportedly came as a result of Mast's family connections to a retired French General, who in turn played a pivotal role in arranging a meeting between Höttl and a French Police Captain named Maurice Blondell. Based in the Austrian city of Bregenz, on the eastern tip of Lake Constance, Blondell was the main conduit into the French agency, and responsible for passing Höttl's information on to his superiors at the DB once a deal was reached. In exchange for that material Blondell was said to have supplied Höttl with false identity papers, which reportedly allowed him to travel unhindered to both Switzerland and Italy. He also authorized Höttl's use of his own Army vehicle for travel into West Germany, thereby greatly enhancing Höttl's ability to transport information. Evidence corroborating these claims was discovered amongst Höttl's private papers at the Austrian National Archives. In a document dated Nov. 28, 1949, and signed by French Sûreté Commissioner, Emil Dabonville, all concerned were advised that official permission had been granted to Messrs. Wilhelm Höttl, Paul Neunteufel, Ottokar Pessl, Fritz Wagner and Karl Neulinger to travel freely within the French controlled jurisdiction around Bregenz. Not only did the document imply the named persons were operating on behalf of the Sûreté, it also created the scenario of Höttl or any of his subordinates having feasibly gained access to secret accounts in Swiss banks. Also worth noting was that the document was written several weeks before Höttl was formally dismissed by the CIC.

Not content with merely two clients in his paddock, Höttl continued to seek alliances with other intelligence services in the European theatre, focusing his efforts at one time or another on the British, Czechs, and even the Soviets. One report supporting suspicions of his eastern contacts, centred on the activities of a woman by the name of Edith Berndt. Known to be the girlfriend of Baron 'Harry' Mast, Berndt just happened to hold strong connections to the Czech Intelligence Service. Concerned over the possible implications that association could have, the Americans decided to increase surveillance on their former underling. Over the next months, the monitoring not only confirmed the 'notorious seller of intelligence information' was plying his trade to the utmost of his ability, but also exposed ties Höttl had built with an organization known as Amt Blank.

Amt Blank had come into existence in 1950 as a result of recommendations submitted to German Chancellor Konrad Adenauer to establish a German defence ministry. Originally titled the Centre for Home Service, the concept had been tolerated by Allied authorities, despite its advocation of German rearmament. Initially under the direction of Gerhard Graf von Schwerin, the Centre was taken over in October by Theodor Blank, the man who later served as West Germany's Defence Minister.

Convinced Höttl had been secretly passing information obtained from Amt Blank on to other interested parties, but lacking any concrete proof, there was little the Americans could do but watch, warn and wait. By mid-1952 however, they felt confident enough to co-ordinate steps to sever all remaining ties between Höttl and all American-run or supported organizations, recommending that other Allied agencies do likewise.

Despite yet another American enjoinder to make him a "persona non grata", Höttl not only managed to maintain his status within the Gehlen Organization, but actually improved on it, convincing an OG agent to have him placed directly on the official payroll. A sign of just how chaotic and intrigue-filled the environment was at the time, it would take three months for the Americans to get wind of Höttl's latest coup, and institute measures to insure that the man who had "successfully convinced one intelligence service after another of his value," was banished from US intelligence circles once and for all.

Ever since the stinging rebuke experienced at the hands of the ÖVP in 1949, Höttl had felt an enduring frustration over his inability to secure a credible forum for what he described as his 'legitimate views'. With direct immersion in the political arena all but ruled out, he was forced to forage for leverage elsewhere, eventually finding it with the Munich-based, nationalist paper, *"Deutsche Soldaten-Zeitung"*(DSZ). Founded by several former SS officers in 1950, the paper was intended to serve as a vehicle that would accurately reflect their political outlook, as well as promoting the written works of former SS colleagues. One of the co-founders of the DSZ was Helmut Damerau, a former NSDAP district leader in East Prussia. Damerau and his associates, Joachim Ruoff, a former General in the Waffen SS, and Heinrich Detloff von Kalben, the former Gauinspektor for Magdeburg-Anhalt, managed to secure backing for their project from Munich's Schild publishing house. On June 6th, 1951, thirty thousand copies of the first issue spilled on to the streets of the Bavarian capital, boasting of standing for *"honour, rights and freedom"* for the man in uniform, and the promotion of *"European Security and loyalty."* As mollifying as that motto may have sounded, there was little doubt about the political territory the trio had staked out for the paper. Over the next months, further evidence of their editorial stance was repeatedly illustrated in a series of nationalistic articles.

Höttl is believed to have joined the DSZ team in the latter half of 1951. Free from the constraints imposed by the lengthy recounting of history in 'The Secret Front', he called upon the journalistic talents honed as a war reporter in Yugoslavia, to begin submitting a number of contemporary articles. Within a relatively short span of time, his prolificacy at the paper resulted in his appointment as the DSZ's Austrian correspondent. Although no samples of his work survive, the fact his tenure extended well into the fall of 1952 leaves the impression his reports had been well received. Despite that approval however, his time with the paper had not been without controversy. Trouble began in June '52, when rumours surfaced about his alleged secret contacts to known Communists. Unlike previous occasions where similar allegations were met by denials or indifference, this time Höttl chose to resign, reportedly taking a number of his *"like-minded"* colleagues along with him. Hoping to downplay a potentially damaging scandal, the board of the Schild Verlag issued a statement distancing itself from its former employee, portraying Höttl as *"merely an occasional freelance co-worker for the paper in Austria"*. The statement went on to describe his departure as the result of having misrepresented himself in the paper's name.

Another DSZ employee caught up in the fray was former Waffen SS General, Felix Martin Steiner. Born on May 23rd. 1896, in Stallupönen, East Prussia, Steiner's military career began as an officer of the German Army in World War I. Following his demobilization in 1919, he became a long-standing member of the Freikorps, joining the NSDAP and SS in 1935. In October of 1936, he was posted to Bad Tolz to serve as a military instructor at the SS Junkerschule. Later transferred to a similar position at the SS school in Dachau, in 1938 he was assigned to a troop contingent as part of the occupation force in Czechoslovakia. Service in Poland and France followed, during which time he volunteered to assist in the establishment of the Waffen SS. Following an extended tour of duty on the Russian Front, Steiner received the unenviable assignment of trying to rescue the doomed city of Berlin in the dying weeks of the war. Unable to accomplish that task, he surrendered to American authorities in May 1945. Whether guilty of serious offences or not, like so many of his high-ranking colleagues, Steiner somehow avoided prosecution and was released after several years in an English POW camp. Once back in Germany, much of his time was devoted to writing books based on his numerous campaigns. Steiner's own ties to the Schild Verlag were a result of his acquaintance with fellow East Prussian 'stalwart', Helmut Damerau. Offered the chance to contribute his expertise to the paper, Steiner remained a member of the Schild Verlag's Advisory Council until December 1952. Given that he had spent a considerable amount of his career flailing against the *"Red Menace"*, it seems unlikely Steiner would have aligned himself with a man suspected of maintaining Communist ties. How many 'like minded colleagues' actually did choose to follow Höttl's departure remains uncertain, but his association with the DSZ does stand as another clear indication of the company he was keeping at the time.

Compared to the career denouements of many former contemporaries, which came at the end of a rope, a jail cell or foreign exile, the demise of Höttl's service in intelligence circles had proven a relatively tranquil affair. While it was claimed that portions of Höttl's voluminous testimony at Nuremberg had contributed to the dispersal of the first two fates, a disturbing number of former high-ranking Nazis managed to achieve the third destiny without his contribution. Some fugitives forced underground by their notoriety had relied on their own devices to flee abroad. Others were able to remain in hiding until arrangements could be organized by one of the illicit 'rescue' operations set up to assist them in reaching sanctuary. Die Schleuse, Kreis Rudel, Stille Hilfe, Bruderschaft, Verband Deutscher Soldaten, Die Spinne and Kameradschaftswerk were just a few of the groups in Germany and Austria that responded to the anticipated post-war 'need', but it was one known as ODESSA which had wielded the most pervasive influence. Organized to assist former SS members threatened with prosecution to escape to safer havens in Latin and South America, ODESSA is thought to have gotten its start sometime in 1948. *"More amateurish than professional"* in the beginning, it was initially comprised of a loose network of small groups whose membership was intentionally limited to guard against infiltration and betrayal. It wasn't until the early 1950's that it matured enough to allow for a larger number of fugitives to have, in Höttl's words *"gone through"*.

Other sources claimed ODESSA's origins went back much further, traceable to a meeting in the Maison Rouge Hotel in Strasbourg on August 12,1944. On that date, government representatives of the Nazi Ministry of Armaments and War Production, and officials from various arms manufacturers such as Heco, Krupp and Röchling, reportedly came together to discuss ways of insuring Germany would retain some level of economic clout after the war. Convinced the war was lost, the group of twelve men attending the 'Strasbourg Conference,' tabled a plan which called for the establishment of a fund to assist German firms in building up their assets and industry in foreign lands. 'Contributions' for the proposed fund were to be garnered from three main sources. The first was the plunder seized from deported and murdered Jews, which according to statistics, had soared into the multiple millions before the end of the war. More than 4.4 tons of gold had flowed into the coffers of the Reichsbank from Auschwitz alone. The second envisioned fount was the vast reserves of Operation Bernhard, theoretically still accessible through its worldwide distribution network. The final *"Quelle"* was the *'donations'* solicited from German businesses interested in increasing prospects for their longevity. The donations were in effect a means for firms to siphon off capital to their foreign subsidiaries,in order to prevent it from being confiscated and used as war reparations by the Allied victors. Told of the feasibility of working through Swiss intermediary banks in Basel and Zurich, *'investors'* were advised how the expanded investment of German capital abroad would also help to create a bulwark against the looming threat of Communist hegemony.

Höttl 1999:
"The money that was there and fed in, was from the German businessmen, industrialists, who supported everything that was against communism. In their own interests, for they knew if the Communists took over they would lose everything.This was a community with the same interests."

In addition to the goal of staving off Communism, the Strasbourg group also agreed to a codicil stipulating that a portion of the collected monies would be made available to the Party. Although not specifically spelled out at the Maison Rouge meeting, the intended purpose of the diverted money was to finance a scheme to assist top Nazi officials escape from what was presumed certain prosecution. In passing the motion, vested interests on both sides of the table recognized the benefits of aiding people with highly incriminating information, to prolong their freedom in a distant land.

Whatever the true nature of ODESSA's beginnings, sources agree its first base of operations was Spain. Grateful for the backing his forces had received from Hitler during the Spanish Civil War, General Francisco Franco's fascist regime did little to discourage the flow of alleged war criminals seeking shelter in his domain.

Höttl: 1999
"Those who did get to Spain felt relatively protected. If the German government issued an extradition order, it was not acted on. Instead of the guilty party being sent back to Germany, he remained living on Spanish soil. After awhile the German diplomats didn't know how to locate their suspects anymore because most no longer went by their own names."

One of those Spanish guests who declined to live incognito was the *"all round Nazi"*, Otto Skorzeny. Skorzeny had escaped to Madrid in 1948, living there under his own name while he established a reputation within the social circles of the Spanish capital. Some sources named him as having been the guiding hand behind ODESSA in its early phase, but Höttl disputed such a claim, pointing out that with his successful businesses and social status, heightened by his marriage to a wealthy socialite, Skorzeny had no need or interest in involving himself in such a dangerous and unprofitable scheme. Others sources made the opposite claim, saying it was precisely because of his social station and business reputation that Skorzeny was able to conceal his secret administration of ODESSA.

With or without Skorzeny at the helm, ODESSA began operating with branches in Madrid and Barcelona. Promoting itself under the banner of *"anti -Communism"*, it quickly developed contacts to Spanish authorities, as well as the intelligence service. As organizational skills gradually improved, the network expanded into other countries, relying on experienced locals to organize a network of 'support points', and serve as contacts for the planned escape routes. The first branch office in Germany was reportedly established at the *"Volkshochschule"* in the city of Coburg. In addition to supplying false documents and setting up a regular courier service between Germany and Spain, the Coburg office was also responsible for carrying out acts of sabotage in the nearby Soviet zone in an attempt to prevent the Russians from dismantling and removing German industrial facilities.

In spite of Höttl's acknowledged close acquaintance with many of the figures involved in post-war rescue operations, he consistently denied having directly participated in them. Despite that claim, he rarely had difficulty delivering a minute depiction of how the operations functioned.

Höttl: 1999

"There were various support spots in Germany, but also in Austria, where people being sought, could make themselves known. They had ashtrays made ... and these ashtrays looked particularly special,... with the image of a church engraved on the underside,... a prominent Church, either the Cologne Cathedral, or in Austria, the Stephan Cathedral in Vienna. They placed these ashtrays on the tables in reliable guesthouses, reliable in the sense as far as National Socialism was concerned, for those who were seeking contact. The "Church" was a signal so they knew 'here I am in the right place. Here I can ask

for help'. The contacts would then say to their counterparts 'we're sending him to you, he wants to get out', and then they would direct him further."

As demand for ODESSA's services gathered momentum, there was a corresponding rise in the need for increased funding and co-ordination. On constant lookout for new sources of support, ODESSA operatives decided to approach the Gehlen Organization, itself already a haven for numerous former Nazis despite American orders banning their recruitment. More than a few professionals within OG's ranks were willing to lend their expertise to the cause at hand, and with OG's assistance, ODESSA envoys were able to secure much needed identity and travel documents. They still however, needed help with the coordination and administrative aspects of the operation. Enter Friedrich Schwend, whose experience with Operation Bernhard made him a welcome candidate to assume control of ODESSA's funding mechanisms.

Schwend's path to ODESSA reportedly began in late 1944, with a proposal to help hinder the establishment of the *'Alpenfestung'*, the much ballyhooed fortress the Nazis were reportedly building within the Alps. Even though Höttl later usurped the plan for his own purposes, it was Schwend who had first broached the idea with American officials. Having gained their interest, he was authorized to travel through areas of German-held territory with the ostensible goal of persuading pockets of resistance to lay down their arms. Shortly before the German collapse precluded the need for further work, Schwend had returned to Meran. He was captured not long after and held by British forces keen on questioning him about his role in Operation Bernhard. When word of his internment reached American officials, they used their influence to gain his release. Schwend immediately departed for Munich, stopping off in the Kaunertal area of western Austria, to allegedly bury millions of fake bank notes. Once in the Bavarian capital, he quickly became involved in the city's flourishing black market. Picked up by American Army Corps Intelligence Division (CID) officials on suspicion of dealing in stolen art in early 1947, he reportedly regained his liberty with the aid of a former OB assistant with contacts inside the CID, and access to OB funds. In the interim, an Italian court had sentenced Schwend in absentia, to 21 years imprisonment for his alleged involvement in the murder of an intelligence agent. Unaware or unconcerned with this development, American officials released their captive a short while later. Once back on

the street, Schwend concluded it unwise to wait around for a possible change of heart and decamped Munich for South America. Settling in the Peruvian capital of Lima, within weeks he had acquainted himself with members
of the exiled Nazi community, one of whom was Klaus Barbie. Together
with other former Nazis, he embarked on a series of dubious business ventures thought to have included arms sales, drug smuggling and stock mani-
pulations, many reportedly financed with OB's vast supply of funds. Schwend
was thought to have had an enormous trove at his disposal. By the end of the
war, the counterfeiting operation had produced over 9 million notes, with a
face value estimated as high as £300 million. Only £130 million had made it
into actual circulation, leaving a sizeable amount still unaccounted for. A
portion had remained in the hands of various OB agents, each of whom was
allowed to keep 15% of the funds they were to convert into real currency. As
various diving expeditions later proved, a large chunk of OB's stockpile also
ended up at the bottom of various lakes within the Salzkammergut, the most
legendary cache in the Toplitzsee. That still left a sizeable amount for
Schwend. Because of the extraordinary quality of the counterfeit notes, he
was reportedly able to continue using OB funds for the well being of former
colleagues on the run, well into the mid- 50's. It was only when the Bank of
England issued a total recall of all ten pound notes to counter the damaging
effects the near perfect bills had had on the British economy, that Schwend's
influence was lessened.

The man believed to have co-chaired ODESSA's financial department
with Schwend, was a Swiss banker by the name of Francois Genoud. In possession of what some sources called impeccable Nazi credentials, Genoud's
ties to the Nazi Party had begun with a chance encounter the 16 year old had
with Adolf Hitler in a Bad Godesberg hotel in 1932. His already fervid Nazi
beliefs welded by that meeting, Genoud joined the pro-Nazi National Front
Party immediately upon his return to Lausanne. Purportedly engaged in
numerous Nazi-related activities during the latter half of the 1930's, he began working for both the Swiss and German Intelligence Services, traveling
extensively and coming in contact with numerous high ranking Nazi officials. While he managed to keep most of these contacts and the activities they
generated in the shadows, Genoud's reputation eventually surfaced through
his work as a publisher of Nazi propaganda, much of which expressed his
strong anti-Jewish sentiments. A long time supporter of Arab nationalism,
Genoud also utilized his network of contacts and resources to curry favour

with various Arab regimes, several of which later offered sanctuary to fleeing SS war criminals. A prime example of Genoud's influence was the case of Eichmann deputy, Alois Brunner, who with ODESSA's assistance was able to find refuge in Syria, living there in relative tranquility until his death in 1992. Genoud's enduring loyalty to the Nazis was also reflected in his having financed the defence teams for both Adolf Eichmann and Klaus Barbie. In 1996 however, circumstances brought him into confrontation with his own past. Deeply implicated in the investigation of Nazis and Swiss collusion over the sequestering of Holocaust victims' assets in secret Swiss accounts, the 81 old year Genoud was not able to rely on a similar patron for assistance, committing suicide at his home in Lausanne before the case came to trial.

Schwend himself, would continue to administer his numerous business dealings and 'aid program' relatively undisturbed for some time. Undisturbed however, did not mean undetected. Under surveillance by Peruvian authorities, he was arrested in 1974 and convicted of illegal stock trading. Sentenced to two years, upon his release he was deported to Bonn where he was immediately arrested by German authorities on the outstanding Italian warrant. Transferred for trial in Munich, he was convicted in 1979 as part of a deal reached with prosecutors. Sentenced to two years on parole and deported back to Peru, he would not see the inside of a jail cell again before dying in Lima in 1980.

Meanwhile back in Europe, in spite of the precautions ODESSA operatives and their counterparts in the Gehlen Organization had taken, the organization's activities had not gone unnoticed by Allied authorities. The Allies however, were reluctant to introduce measures to hinder the operation, largely because the CIC was busy using its own resources to spirit what it considered to be 'valuable people' out of Europe, to keep them from falling into Soviet hands. After it became apparent many of the individuals the US was prepared to assist were too hot to handle through normal channels, American interests often coalesced with ODESSA's goals and OG's capabilities.

Höttl 1999:
"At that time the American intelligence organs often knew what was going on, but their attitude was 'this man is important for us so we don't want to know what was with him'. I experienced this a considerable number of times,

and was told quite matter of factly, ' he has such a good connection with Russia, ... it is of no importance to us, what he was'".

As active as ODESSA and the US Intelligence services had been in rationalizing and rallying support for their cause, another powerful institution was proving to be just as willing to provide sustenance for its followers, be they suspected war criminals or not.

To the average observer, the idea of a respected organization modifying its principles to facilitate the harbouring and transporting of suspected war criminals would seem to border on the incomprehensible. Yet despite evidence that such a practice was tolerated, if not sanctioned by the Vatican in the years after World War II, many have chosen to dismiss such a prospect as nothing more than anti-Church propaganda. What prompted the Holy See's unholy collaboration to a large extent laid with its overt abhorrence of all things Communist.

The Church's first anti-Communist actions appear to have emerged in the 1930's, when various elements of its congregation banded together to form what became known as the *"Intermarium"*. Translated as *"between the seas"*, Intermarium's mandate was to organize a number of anti-Communist groups in Eastern Europe with the goal of uniting people against the threat posed by the atheistic regime of the Soviet Union. After the outbreak of war in 1939, stemming the encroaching red menace took on even more importance, spurring many of Intermarium's members to develop ties with various fascist regimes in power at the time. As a result, clerics began to wield a noticeable degree of influence within various government circles. Such was the case in Slovakia, Croatia, and Hungary, all of which possessed large Catholic populations. While it must be said that numerous leading Church figures did use their positions to protest against Nazi aggression and persecution, there were those who chose to overlook 'regrettable policies' if the overall activities of fascist leaders ultimately helped further the Church's fight against Communism. Such a stance inevitably led to a number of controversial decisions the Church ostensibly made on behalf of its *'flock'*. One contentious measure was initiated in late 1944, as the Third Reich was entering its final descent. Utilizing Intermarium's network of contacts, sundry Church representatives began implementing plans to aid Catholic refugees fleeing from the advancing Soviet army. While the majority qualified as potential victims of religious or political persecution, others were avid Nazis or their collaborators, using the available mechanism to evade facing justice. The Church sponsored system was easy to abuse as to a large extent all that was required to be eligible for assistance was a professed stance of being anti-Communist. This policy of flexible tolerance had continued after hostilities ceased in May

1945, as evidenced by Intermarium's call for the release of Waffen SS prisoners-of war to help build an army of anti-Communists.

There was no shortage of willing confederates to aid the Church in its crusade. Agencies such as the CIC and the Gehlen Organization were at the forefront, maintaining hiring practises that clearly demonstrated how anything redolent of anti-Communism covered the scent of more odious activities. Much as they had done with OG, officials within the American Intelligence community decided to explore the potential for co-operation with Intermarium in dealing with *"special refugees"* too sensitive to handle themselves. Rather than approaching Church officials directly, the Americans turned to their proteges at the Gehlen Organization. To help foster links with the Church, OG agents in turn enlisted the services of Licio Gelli, a man already well acquainted with the various rescue operations.

Born in Pistoia, Tuscany on April 21st, 1919, Gelli had been a *'cardinal'* candidate for the job at hand. A volunteer Italian *"Black Shirt"* who fought alongside Franco's troops in the Spanish Civil War, and was a close associate of Italian Fascist dictator, Benito Mussolini, Gelli had at one time served as a liaison officer to the German Reich, a platform he used to become familiar with many of the top Nazi elite. As the purported head of the secret Masonic Lodge P2 in his own country, Gelli made use of his numerous contacts to establish links to the man responsible for setting up one of the first functioning escape channels.

Krunoslav Stjepan Draganovic was born in the city of Travnik, 90 kilometres west of Sarajevo, in 1903. After completing his education in the Bosnia-Herzegovina capital and Vienna, he went on to a Professorship of Theology at the University of Zagreb. Taking a sabbatical from that position in 1932, Draganovic traveled to Rome to carry out post-graduate studies at the Papal Oriental Institute, while working part time at the Vatican Archives. He returned to Yugoslavia in 1935, and shortly thereafter became private secretary to the Archbishop of Sarajevo, Ivan Saric, a fierce Croatian nationalist and early supporter of the fascist Ustascha Party. His close proximity to the fanatical priest over the next six years had an indelible impact on him. In 1941 when Ustascha leader, Ante Pavelic declared Croatia an independent entity, Draganovic followed in Saric's footsteps by becoming an ordained priest and officially swearing his allegiance to the fascist party. Subsequently appointed Vice President of the Ustascha's Office for Colonization, little more than a pseudonym for the ethnic cleansing waged against thousands of Serbs and Jews during the war, Draganovic played a crucial role in the forced conversion of Orthodox Serbs to Catholicism. He was also suspected of having overseen the seizure of assets from victims deported or murdered under the Ustascha regime.

At the urging of the Ustascha leadership, in 1943 the Croatian Church sent Draganovic back to Rome to serve as the representative for the International Red Cross. Although the position was nothing more than a front to carry out intelligence activities on behalf of the Ustascha, Draganovic used the opportunity to broaden what was already a substantial list of acquaintances, reported to have even included Pope Pius XII. In early 1945, he accepted promotion to Secretary of the Croatian Institute at the College of San Girolamo degli Illrici. Within months, he introduced 'prescient' measures to adapt San Girolamo into a sanctuary for fleeing Ustascha leaders, measures which reportedly received the silent acknowledgement of both Institute leader, Monsignor Juraj Magjerec and Pope Pius XII himself. One of the first to take advantage of the San Girolamo refuge was Ustascha leader, Ante Pavelic. Captured and held in Austria by the British Army's 5th Corps shortly after the close of the war, Pavelic reportedly negotiated his freedom with portions of the treasure in his possession at the time of arrest. After purportedly handing over some $3 million in gold coins to unidentified authorities, Pavelic, former police chief Andrija Artkovic, and others in the Ustascha entourage were given safe passage to Italy, where another large segment of Pavelic's illicit wealth was thought to have changed hands at San Girolamo, before he was able to flee to Argentina two years later.

Backed with similar 'fees' collected from other war criminals, Draganovic's 'Ratline' quickly expanded beyond its Ustascha clientele to include other 'Catholics' in need. In response to the growing demand for their services, he and Vatican officials reportedly contacted Cardinals throughout the world to have them persuade government leaders to grant sanctuary for Catholic ex-Nazis with strong anti-Communist leanings. High on the list of sympathetic patrons were the leaders of various countries in Latin and South America.

As a result of preliminary negotiations held between Draganovic and Gelli in the summer of 1947, the Gehlen Organization agreed to collaborate on the use of future 'Ratlines'. Among the new roads destined to lead to Rome was the so-called "Monastery Route", instituted between Austria and Italian capital in mid-1948. Although Draganovic and his associates were responsible for setting up the infrastructure for the new trail, running it would not have been feasible were it not for the cooperation of Bishop Alois Hudal. Often thought to have been of Slovenian descent, Alois Hudal was in fact born in Graz, Austria on May 31, 1885. After completing his education in the city of his birth, Hudal was ordained as a priest in 1908, going on to obtain his Doctorate of Theology three years later. Between 1911 and 1913, his time was devoted to post-graduate studies in Rome, at the end of which he returned home to Austria to accept a professorship at Graz University. He would hold that tenure for almost nine years, before moving back to Rome to take over as Rector of the Pontifical Teutonic College at Santa Maria del ANIMA, a foundation established to provide support and accommodation for German and Austrian priests studying in Rome. Hudal's duties at ANI-MA included serving as priest confessor to the German speaking community, as well as an official advisor to the Pope. An ardent nationalist and anti-Semite, Hudal had greeted the rise of the Nazis in Germany and Austria, praising their policies in his 1936 book, *"The Basis of NS"*, an act of devotion that earned him the NSDAP's Golden badge of honour. Höttl claimed to have first crossed paths with Hudal in 1943, while serving as Italian Referat in Rome. Portraying him as *"open, worldly and charming"*, and not the rigid 'Church man' one might have expected for someone in his position, Höttl acknowledged Hudal's fierce and unconditional opposition to anything connected to Communism.

Hudal:
"I support everything that is against Communism and I can't ask to know what a man had for a past. What's important for me is what he did against communism and what he will do against it."

Following the German surrender in Italy in April 1945, Hudal began familiarizing himself with 'candidates for rescue' during visits he made to German-speaking prisoner of war camps. The visits spurred him to learn more about activities reportedly being undertaken by some of his fellow clergyman. In his book, *"Confessions of an Old Priest"*, published posthumously in 1976, Hudal recounted his subsequent commitment to Draganovic's operations, boasting that of all the *"charitable work"* undertaken during this period, nothing had been of greater importance to him than helping many SS members, fascists and war criminals escape their potential tormentors.

While shared sympathies may have been the motivation behind Hudal's work with Draganovic, few of his actions would have been possible without the tacit support of his superior, Pope Pius XII. Also fundamentally averse to Bolshevism, Eugenio Pacelli's apparent acquiescence towards Hudal's adventures was derived from his own strong affection for the German people, developed while serving as the Vatican's Nuncio in Munich and Berlin during the 1920's. Pacelli's attitude towards the Nazis was also influenced by the cabal of German priests that surrounded him following his rise to the papacy in March of 1939. Many of those same figures had previously been under Hudal's tutelage in the early 30's, before becoming ardent supporters of National Socialism upon their return to Germany. Friends with Hudal since 1924, Pius XII was prepared to back his Bishop, after Hudal made it clear *"something needed to be done"* to save Nazi Catholics from Allied vengeance, i.e. Communist reprisals. Precisely how many *'Catholic'* Nazis Hudal and his colleagues helped escape remains speculative. Estimates have soared as high as 20,000, but Höttl claimed a figure between two and three thousand was more realistic. Statistics were not the only element of the Ratlines Höttl was familiar with. Although he claimed his extensive knowledge was the result of astute observation rather than participation, for someone purportedly on the sidelines, he possessed an inordinate amount of details on how the operation functioned in Austria.

Höttl: 1999

"The second last station was in an ordinary old house in the middle of Innsbruck. Care was taken so that it wouldn't appear conspicuous, so people could sleep for a day or two. From there the people got over the border into South Tyrol where they were received by people from Bishop Hudal. Most were then housed in monasteries… It wasn't always possible that a ship would be sailing for Spain and later on to South America, so the people had to wait and be taken care of in monasteries. With authentic documents they were later taken out of Italy to Spain."

Two other clerics involved at the time in reshaping Nazi futures were Father Dominik Mandic and Father Josef Gallov. Mandic, a Bosnian member of the Franciscan order, had been responsible for administering the financial resources of the operations, while Gallov, a Hungarian priest, played a central role in obtaining and distributing the false identity papers needed to obtain genuine Red Cross travel visas. Some sources claimed the fake documents originated from the Vatican Refugee Organization, while others contended they came from the offices of a former CIC officer named Robert Bishop, responsible for running the International Refugee Office in Rome. Whatever the source, the allegations are another example of the level of co-operation that existed amongst all interested parties.

Höttl: 1999

"The French Occupation Force was there in Austria but they didn't know anything about this. The Americans had worked together at the higher level, but in this case they didn't want to know all the details. In Italy, the police and the military were strongly anti-communist and supported everything that was done in this cause. They knew that some of the people had warrants out on them, and should have been extradited, but all of this was suppressed, and they allowed these fugitives the freedom to travel with their passports to Rome... Bishop Hudal became the most important person because he could do everything. He had the connections to the Italian authorities and could obtain Italian emigration papers, so they were in effect legalized. That was the most important thing because there were control checkpoints everywhere."

In a belated attempt to cast Hudal in a better light, Höttl claimed the escape routes had not been open to everyone and that efforts, however limited, were made to filter candidates as they passed through the system. According to Höttl, the 'refugees' were required to complete a resumé during their stay at a monastery, but with almost no way of verifying the information, decisions were usually made in favour of the candidate. With the threat of infiltration by enemy intelligence agencies always hovering, agents in Austria also endeavoured to vet an individual's identity prior to sending him on his way, a duty for which Höttl was particularly well suited.

Höttl 1999:

"People formerly in the intelligence service were asked if the man was known, or if this was his true identity. These were people with experience, trained secret service officers who made themselves available, and as experts could naturally verify someone faster and better as a layman."

For many of the shipments cleared by these assessors, the countries of South America were favoured destinations, not only because of the obliging attitudes of ruling dictators, but also the attraction of being able to submerge within the large ex-patriot communities. This latter appeal was particularly true in the case of Argentina, where some 60,000 German ex-patriates in Buenos Aires alone, had joined the NSDAP prior to the war. Much to the fortune of fleeing Nazis, the Argentine government at the time had been under the control of General Juan Peron. Akin to Eugenio Pacelli, Peron had also harboured a great sympathy for Germany and its people, having served there as a military envoy in the late 1930's.

Höttl: 1999
"It didn't matter what sort of past a man might have had to Peron. What was important was whether or not the man was clearly anti-communist. He had used a lot of these people from Europe to begin his own intelligence service, people who were guaranteed anti-Communists. Whether the man was a war criminal or not was of no interest to Peron... Evita Peron was especially active in assisting fugitives. When very attractive men appeared, if she liked them, then she helped them, irregardless of what they had done."

◆

The list of suspected criminals ultimately able to take advantage of the *'Ratlines'* was disturbingly long. Hovering near the top of that register was the notorious Angel of Death, who with a flick of his wrist had sent thousands to their death in Auschwitz. After four years in hiding as a farmhand near Rosenheim, Bavaria, Josef Mengele was smuggled to the Italian port city of Genoa in 1949, after an old friend managed to make contact with locals running the *'Ratline'*. Once in Genoa he was supplied with a Red Cross passport made out in the name of Helmut Gregor, and quickly bundled off to the relative safety of Brazil. Over the next few years, he found it prudent to change residences numerous times in order to stay ahead of his pursuers, but in 1959 felt secure enough to apply for Paraguayan citizenship under his own name. Eventually forced to flee that country, he landed back in Brazil where under the new name of Wolfgang Gerhart, he befriended a Brazilian/German couple by the name of Bossert. Although de-classified reports reveal that American intelligence officials knew of Mengele's whereabouts for some time, for some reason no action was undertaken to apprehend him. As a result, the notorious Nazi doctor was able to live in relative freedom for another two decades before suffering a stroke and drowning at a Sao Paolo beach in 1979. Following up on reports he was buried in the nearby town of Embu, Brazilian authorities launched a forensic investigation of the remains. When first results proved severely flawed, German, American and Israeli governments subsequently sent their own teams of investigators, who were able to confirm the bones were indeed those of Mengele.

Two other infamous Nazis known to have availed themselves of the 'Ratline's' amenities were Franz Stangl, former commandant of the extermination camps at Sobibór and Treblinka, and Klaus Barbie, Gestapo chief of Lyon. Stangl had been transferred to the internment camp at Glasenbach, following his arrest in Bad Ischl in 1945. Somehow able to conceal his death camp activities from officials there, he was tried and sentenced to two years for his role as superintendent of the T-4 euthanasia program in Austria. Fearing his other crimes might one day come to light, Stangl escaped from a Linz prison in May 1948, and made his way to Rome using the facilities of the Monastery Route. Able to acquire a new passport and Red Cross travel visa with the help of Bishop Hudal, he travelled to Syria. Joined there by his wife in 1949, the couple spent the next three years in Damascus before departing for Brazil, again with the reported aid of Hudal's far reaching network. Tracked down and arrested in 1967 thanks to the work of Nazi hunter Simon Wiesenthal, Stangl was extradited to Germany and put on trial for the deaths of over 900,000 people. Convicted and sentenced to life imprisonment in October 1970, eight months later he was found dead in his Düsseldorf prison cell, a victim of heart failure.

Barbie's career and route into exile had been much more circuitous, starting with his posting to the SD's Amt VI France contingent in 1940. From there he had moved on to stints in Amsterdam, Berlin and Dijon before being dispatched to Lyon in November 1942, to deal with 70,000 Jewish refugees who had fled to the city from other parts of German-occupied Europe. As a result of the subsequent atrocities carried out against the Jewish population and core of French resistance fighters, the Gestapo chief earned the title of "Butcher of Lyon". Arrested by British authorities in 1945, Barbie's experience in counter-insurgency tactics induced both British and

American intelligence officials to shield him from prosecution, hoping to use his expertise to suppress leftist movements active in various European countries. Despite being acutely aware of his Nazi past, the Americans also reportedly recruited him as an agent in the 66th detachment of the CIC, a posting that is believed to have lasted until 1955. No longer in need of his services, the Americans assisted Barbie and his family in moving to La Paz, Bolivia. Once in South America, Barbie adopted the name Klaus Altmann. Thanks to a series of lucrative black market activities, he was able to lead a relatively comfortable existence until being tracked down in 1971 by Nazi hunters Serge and Beate Klarsfeld. Despite the discovery of his whereabouts however, Barbie remained free until 1984, at which time a newly elected government in Bolivia decided to deport him to face justice in France. Tried, convicted and sentenced to life imprisonment in 1987, 'the butcher' met his end in a French prison cell four years later.

As dismaying as these various tales of 'unjust rescue' had been, there was one assisted odyssey even more disturbing. Re-tracing the steps that led to Adolf Eichmann's ultimate fate in Jerusalem, it is clear that his flight from Germany had been prompted by testimony emerging from the Nuremberg trials. As one of Eichmann's former top deputies, SS Major Dieter Wisliceny, had provided prosecutors with minute details on the evolution of Nazi plans to resolve the *"Jewish question"*. Up until 1940, *"official"* policy on removing Jews from the Reich had focused largely on forced emigration. The second phase had involved the establishment of ghettos in Poland and other occupied territories in the East, meant to house the 're-settled' Jews. The third phase, or *"final solution"*, was the planned extermination of the Jewish population of Europe, introduced at the Wannsee Conference in January 1942. Although the names of various perpetrators and facilitators were scattered throughout Wisliceny's testimony, it was Eichmann who figured prominently in all three phases of the program.

Within days of Wisliceny's statements, reports had reverberated all across Germany and Austria, even seeping down into the prison population of Allied internment camps. Housed at one US facility was a low-ranking soldier by the name of *"Otto Eckmann"*. In custody since his capture in Austria in May 1945, Eckmann was fearful the Nuremberg testimony would sooner or later be connected with his own person. Assisted by several fellow prisoners, he managed to escape, fleeing north to the Lüneberger Heide, where he reportedly hid out on a farm fifty miles south of Hamburg. Aware the search for his whereabouts had greatly intensified, Eckmann would mutate into Otto Heninger, remaining ensconced on the farm for four years, while avoiding any direct contact with his family in Alt Aussee.

Höttl: 1999

"*I knew her (Eichmann's wife Vera) quite well when she lived here with the children... The whole time she was still here in Alt Aussee, she had no idea what was up with him*".

During her husband's time on the farm, Vera Eichmann showed no signs of having known of his whereabouts. In 1947 however, she abruptly initiated steps to have her missing partner declared legally dead. Brandishing an affidavit from a man named Karl Lukas, later exposed as her brother-in-law, she referred authorities to several witnesses who claimed her husband had been killed in Prague. Aware that Höttl's testimony placed Eichmann in Alt Aussee several weeks after his alleged death, American officials dismissed the petition as nothing more than an attempt to thwart further investigations into Eichmann's whereabouts. In the meantime, rumours over his actual fate continued to swirl, including a reported sighting at the Grundlsee in 1949, that turned out to be Eichmann's brother.

In May 1950, Eichmann was able to make contact with representatives of ODESSA. Thanks to the organization's improved efficiency, within weeks he was en route to the Italian port city of Genoa, reportedly stopping briefly in Bad Goisern, Austria to pick up forged identity papers, before heading for the nearby Gosau See to make his way across the Alps.

Höttl 1999:

"*For people who aren't aware of the connections, it is nearly impossible to understand, how such a thing was possible.*"

Once in Genoa, Eichmann was given shelter in a monastery run by Father Anton Weber of the St. Raphael Society. Making use of the considerable resources at their disposal, Eichmann's 'helpers' secured him a letter of recommendation from the Papal Relief Organization, as well as a Red Cross humanitarian passport in the name of Ricardo Klement. Outfitted with such documentation, there was little difficulty acquiring an official travel visa for Argentina. Within a matter of days, Eichmann was onboard a ship bound for South America.

As with many post-war Nazi sagas, versions as to what happened next tended to vary. One suggested scenario had Eichmann whisked out of Buenos Aires shortly after his arrival on July 14th, and taken to San Miguel de Tucamen, a city 600 miles to the west. There with the help of other SS fugitives, he proceeded to dissolve into relative obscurity, landing work as a supervisor in a water company. A second version had him remaining in Buenos Aires, given refuge and employment through a network of local ex-SS contacts in a nearby town. Over the next two years, he allegedly worked at a series of menial jobs, including spells as a sales representative, laundry assistant, and labourer on a rabbit farm. Whatever the case, by 1952, he felt secure enough in his surroundings to risk making contact with his family. Just after Easter that year, Vera Eichmann obtained a passport in her maiden name from the consular office in Graz. Shortly thereafter, she departed Alt Aussee with her three sons, Klaus, Horst and Dieter, reportedly using the same resources as her husband had two years earlier. Booked passage for Argentina, the family arrived in Buenos Aires on July 28th. Assuming the identity of Catalina Klement, she and her re-united family settled into a modest home in a Buenos Aires suburb not far from her husband's new job at an automobile factory.

Aside from various members of the exiled Nazi community aware of the stranger in their midst, Eichmann remained a nonentity to both neighbours and co-workers. Despite his relative anonymity, reports suggest numerous people in Europe had been on his trail since as far back as 1951. One of them was famed Nazi hunter, Simon Wiesenthal. Not long after having written a series of articles about post-war events in Ausseerland, Wiesenthal had reportedly been visited by a man introducing himself as Heinrich von Klimrod. Claiming to be acting on behalf of a group of former Vienna SS officers, Klimrod proposed to help track Eichmann down in exchange for information they believed Wiesenthal had on his abandoned gold. Sensing the overture a hoax, Wiesenthal dismissed the offer outright, but took it as an indication Eichmann was still alive.

Another clue as to Eichmann's whereabouts surfaced in 1953, when Höttl's associate, Baron "Harry" Mast, contacted Wiesenthal with a letter claiming the fugitive was to be found in Buenos Aires. For some reason no action was taken to investigate Mast's claim.

Four years later, Fritz Bauer, the State Prosecutor for the German State of Hessen, received a letter from a Jewish emigrant by the name of Lother Herrmann. According to Herrmann, Eichmann was residing at Chacobuco Street 4261 in the Olivos suburb of Buenos Aires, something he had learned as a result of his daughter's having recently become acquainted with one of Eichmann's sons. Fearing that commencing official proceedings for Eichmann's extradition might provide the opportunity for him to escape, Bauer chose to pass the information on to Mossad agents in Israel. US documents de-classified in June of 2006, show the information was also given to American officials, who in turn, most likely shared it with the German Intelligence Service (BND). Critics later claimed the BND had requested that no action be undertaken, a move presumably motivated by a fear of what Eichmann might have to say about former Nazis now in important positions within the West German government. One person reportedly at risk from a potentially talkative Eichmann was Hans Globke, a former high ranking bureaucrat in the Interior Ministry during the Nazi reign. Despite reports he had written directives, portions of which were later integrated into the infamous Nazi Race Laws, Globke had managed to continue his political career after the war, rising to become a member of Chancellor Konrad Adenauer's inner circle.

The American intelligence community also did not display any overt interest in picking up Eichmann's trail. Their active involvement in the chase would not occur until late 1959, when as a result of a series of interrogations with former RSHA employees, more information on Eichmann's possible whereabouts was made available. Although there is no record of Höttl having been formally interrogated during this time, as a former high ranking member of the SD, and acknowledged acquaintance of the fugitive, he would have been a prime candidate for questioning.

Finally, after having spent years following up on Fritz Bauer's original tip, on May 11th, 1960, Israeli agents took matters into their own hands, snatching the suspected war criminal off the streets of Buenos Aires and returning him to Israel to face justice.

◆

As for the fates of those who helped Nazi perpetrators prolong their freedom, Draganovic continued offering his ' valued expertise on Eastern

European affairs' well into the 1950's, despite having appeared on a list of war criminals sought by Yugoslav authorities. Such was his perceived usefulness at the time, the Americans reportedly made him an official agent of the CIC, complete with code name *"Dynamo"*. Excused from his duties at the Vatican in 1958, Draganovic remained in the good graces of the Americans for nearly a decade. In the late 60's he re- surfaced in his homeland to denounce his former allies in the Ustascha. While some sources believe his *"change of heart"* prompted Yugoslav officials to allow him to retire to a monastery near Sarajevo until his death in 1983, others saw a different clarification for his granted immunity. Discovered in a memo written by US Army agent, William Gowen, was the assessment that any extradition of Draganovic to face charges would have dealt *"a staggering blow to the Catholic Church"*.

Alois Hudal's functionality turned out to be considerably shorter than that of his Croatian colleague. *'Persuaded'* by Vatican officials to submit his resignation after news of his post-war activities created a public scandal, Hudal vacated his post as Director of ANIMA on July 19, 1952, and was replaced by Bishop Jakob Weinbacher, the former private secretary to the so-called *"Nazi Cardinal"*, Theodor Innitzer. Other than devoting time to write a series of unrepentant memoirs, all that is known about *"the old priest"* after his fall from grace, was that he chose to stay on in a small town near Rome, until his death there on May 13th, 1963.

♦

Taken en masse, his lengthy friendship with Eichmann, the close working relationship with Friedrich Schwend, his *"good standing"* with Bishop Hudal, a familiarity with members of the Ustascha, the numerous contacts within the CIC and Gehlen Organization, his physical proximity and detailed knowledge of the *'Ratline'*, and finally his self-trumpeted loyalty as a Catholic and firm anti-Communist, the question is not so much whether, but rather why, Höttl wouldn't have been involved in the rescue activities.

In the first five years that followed the war, it was estimated that assorted courts managed to identify and charge over 100,000 suspected Nazi *"Täter"*. Of that total however, only 6500 were found guilty, 166 of whom received life sentences. Considering the range and magnitude of crimes carried out under the Nazis, the paltry conviction rate raised the question as to what became of the thousands and thousands of other accomplices who helped the system function? While many were able to rely on various resources to make good their escape, others simply returned to normal lives, often evading justice by minimizing their roles to officials who lacked the proper resources to investigate them all. Almost overnight, thousands of lawyers, businessmen, doctors, army officials, civil servants and policemen were transformed into self-declared victims, convinced the relative leniency shown them had been fully merited.

Signs of the rapid re-integration were everywhere. By the 1950's, fifty percent of the higher ranking staff at the German Foreign Office were confirmed as having been NSDAP members, categorized by Allied investigators as *"Mitläufer"* or 'hangers on'. Similar scenarios were repeated across all segments of German and Austrian society. As unjust as that development was for the many victims of Nazi rule, an even more indefensible specimen of post-war justice was about to occur.

Following the conclusion of the major war criminals trial in October 1946, a series of secondary trials had gotten underway under the supervision of American prosecutors. The first of twelve held between 1946 and 1949, saw twenty-three SS doctors and scientists placed before a US Military Tribunal. Of the sixteen found guilty, seven were later hanged. On September 15th, 1947, it was the turn of former SS special commando group leaders. Fourteen of the twenty-one accused were convicted and sentenced to death, but only four were executed, with the other sentences commuted to life imprisonment. The twelfth and final process, known as the Wilhelmstrasse trial, witnessed four former Ministers, seven former State Secretaries and numerous other high-ranking civil servants tried for their offences. Ernst von Weizsäcker, Edmund Veesenmayer and Walter Schellenberg were amongst the twenty-one arraigned. All but two were found guilty of at least one charge, with sentences ranging from three to twenty-five years.

Höttl 1999:

"Veesenmayer was sentenced to 10 years by an American court and was released after three years. (Ed. note: The original sentence was 20 years, later reduced to 10) That happened with the whole top ranks. The Americans had imposed this great sentence of 20 years, and then the people were set free after 3 or 4 years. I even know of one case where it was 100 years ... and after three years he was released and he obtained a good economic position in Germany."

The roots of what came to be known as the General Amnesty of 1951, were largely attributed to the shifting priorities within the geopolitical arena. One of the first public signs that a drive was underway to alter the terms of justice meted out at Nuremberg, came with the formation of the Heidelberger jurists circle. Consisting primarily of practising lawyers, the circle was conceived in the spring of 1949 as a co-ordinating centre for those factions interested in seeing the 'so called war criminals' freed. Despite the fact the persons in question had been tried and convicted in a court of law, various individuals and forums drew a distinction between *'political'* war criminals and what they referred to as the 'real ones'.

Adding to the brewing storm was public resentment over what many viewed as victor's justice, which by the middle of 1950, had spread to all levels of German society. Even the German Evangelical Church took a stand, stepping forward to present a memorandum calling for a reduction in the sentences of those Germans still in jail. In office for only nine months when the war criminal issue started receiving increased precedence, the American High Commissioner for Germany, John J. McCloy, responded to the Church's request by reducing each sentence by five days a month for good behaviour. Spurred by that partial success, elements of the amnesty movement turned their focus on gaining support from the German Federal government in Bonn. Keenly aware of the widespread desire in the population to *"put the war behind them"*, as well as the political capital to be made by endorsing the goal of reducing the number of Germans still *"domiciled with the Western powers"*, Chancellor Konrad Adenauer was receptive to meeting with representatives of the various groups pushing for amnesty. Parallel to that gesture, was Adenauer's recognition of the opportunity to take advantage of the changes Cold War tensions were bringing to American security policy in Europe. As a consequence, Bonn officials were authorized to petition McCloy for the release of various convicted Nazis, on grounds their services and experience were urgently needed to secure the fledging democracy of West Germany in the fight against increasing Communist influence.

Höttl: 1999
"When the conflict with Russia began, the Americans changed
from one day to the next and said we need the Germans as partners and we can't upset them. That was the big turning point, the Russian politics."

Support for Adenauer's appeal also came from HIAG, a group primarily made up of former SS and Army officers. HIAG campaigned for the release of imprisoned colleagues on the premise they could provide expertise to the US sanctioned plan of establishing a 500,000 man German Army to serve as a deterrent to the Soviets. Two of Hitler's former top Generals, Adolf Ernst Heusinger, and Hans Speidel, now both military advisors to Adenauer, put forward similar arguments. Heusinger, who under the code name of *"Horn"* worked closely with the Gehlen Organization, and Speidel, who later became the first German commander of NATO in Europe, eventually went on to regain their former ranks within that rebuilt German Army.

While halting the threat of advancing Communism was presented as the government's main concern, the desire to restore Germany's reputation in the world at large had been of equal importance to Adenauer. The first step towards accomplishing that task laid in the rehabilitation of the administrative and economical elite, whose honour, influence, and stature, Adenauer felt, continued to be defamed by the incarceration of some of its members. The German President, Theodor Heuss, added to the pressure by writing to Commissioner McCloy, inferring that nothing less than the future of the German republic was at stake if no pardons were granted or more executions carried out.

As a former head of the World Bank and advisor to Presidents Roosevelt and Truman, McCloy was no stranger to making controversial decisions. While serving as Assistant Secretary of the US Army in 1943, he had been largely responsible for the decision to place US citizens of Japanese ancestry into internment camps. In mid-1944, he was assigned to advise

American officials on the feasibility of bombing the *"facilities"* at Auschwitz or the rail lines leading to them.

John McCloy 1944:

"After a study, it is clear that such an operation could be executed only by the diversion of considerable air support essential to the success of our forces now engaged in decisive operations elsewhere... there has been considerable opinion to the effect that such an effort, even if practicable would provoke more vindictive action by the Germans."

From the perspective of those already at or destined for Auschwitz, it is difficult to imagine what might have been more vindictive than a gas chamber and crematorium. Ultimately accepted by military leaders, McCloy's decision generated even more controversy when it was later disclosed a number of Flying Fortress aircraft, awaiting assignment on Italian airfields, had in fact been available for such a bombing raid.

McCloy hesitated in delivering a direct response to Adenauer's petition, believing that any changes in the status of war criminals needed to be balanced between the exaggerated hopes of the German people, and the concerns of American citizens with little desire to see the convicted freed.

John McCloy 1950:

"I do wish that the German government and the German people had a wider concept of the crimes which are represented by many of those at Landsberg. I find from my mail, the most abysmal ignorance of both the offences, and the character of the proof of the guilt which prevails in respect to them. I hope to improve this situation to some degree by issuing a rather complete report on the matter simultaneously with my decisions. To some extent this will not make pleasant reading but I feel the current misunderstandings compel, it."

In seeking a middle ground, McCloy announced plans for the creation of a 'Pardon Commission'. Scheduled to begin work in the summer of 1950, the three man panel was to review all cases tried at Nuremberg and report its findings to the State department within 60 days. That at least was the plan. Unable to gain the necessary support for his proposed commission, as an interim solution, McCloy decided to introduce a 'Clemency Panel' with himself as chairman. After conducting an accelerated review of what it called the *'just convictions'* of Nuremberg, the panel concluded that redu-cing the sentences by a third would best serve both parties. The decision, which was implemented retroactively, resulted in the release of a number of prominent Nazis in August of 1950.

Although initially encouraged by McCloy's measures, two months la-ter the German government felt plans for further releases had stalled. Ho-ping to goad the Americans into action, Adenauer wrote to McCloy in No-vember, requesting that all war crime trials be suspended or ended as quickly as possible, pardons be granted in the widest possible spectrum, and all ex-traditions ceased immediately. McCloy's response was facilitated by the fact that by the winter of 1950/51, the Americans had all but retreated from their wartime promise to seek out and try Nazi criminals.

Meanwhile, the much delayed 'Pardon Commission' had come to life, occupying itself with a review of the hundred and two remaining prisoners at Landsberg. On January 31st 1951, it published its findings, recommen-ding that fifty-two of fifty-four standing sentences be reduced. For thir-ty-two of those prisoners, that translated into immediate release. In additi-on, twenty-one of twenty-eight men on death row saw their sentences commuted. Despite massive pressure to rescind the remaining death sen-tences, on June 8th, SS Major General Otto Ohlendorf, former leader of Einsatzgruppe D and self-admitted murderer of over 95,000 people, and SS Lt. General Oswald Pohl, the man responsible for instituting the concept of slave labor at concentration camps were hanged at Landsberg. The majority of the remaining seventy-nine prisoners were freed within several months.

The fates of the released individuals, many of whom were former asso-ciates or acquaintances of Höttl, differed. SS Lt. General Erich von dem Bach-Zelewski, commander of the forces that brutally put down the Warsaw Ghetto uprising, and assisted in the overthrow of the Hungarian Horthy regime in 1944, was originally sentenced to 10 years but set free as part of the amnesty in 1951. Re-arrested in 1961 he, was subsequently found guilty of the 1933 murder of three Communists and sentenced to life imprison-ment. He died in a Munich jail in 1972.

Höttl's former mentor, SS Brigadier General Heinz Jost, leader of an Ein-satzgruppe, before becoming the Plenipotentiary for the Baltic States and parts of White Russia, was sentenced to life imprisonment in 1948. Although the sentence was later reduced to ten years, Jost too was released in 1951, sett-ling in Düsseldorf, where he worked in real estate until his death in 1964.

Another Einsatzgruppe commander freed by the amnesty was SS Brigadier General, Dr. Franz Six. Convicted on charges his unit had killed 15,000 people behind the Eastern Front, Six was sentenced to twenty years in 1948. Released in 1952 after serving less than four years, he returned to southern Germany, where he purchased a publishing company and became the media advisor to several well known German firms. Also believed to have joined the ranks of the Gehlen Organization, Six moved to the northern town of Bad Harzburg in 1963, to accept a position at a nearby Academy, lecturing on the 'leadership qualities' needed for the marketplace. Able to see out his career as a business consultant, he died while vacationing at his summer home in South Tyrol in 1975.

Höttl's former supervisor and head of Amt VI, SS Brigadier General Walter Schellenberg was also a beneficiary of the general amnesty. Although convicted of having been a member of the SS and SD, rather than being sent to jail, Schellenberg spent the next year shunting between various hospitals and clinics in hopes of improving his failing health. Released in December of 1950, he initially moved to Switzerland, before eventually settling in Turin. Suffering from severe gall bladder problems as well as liver hepatitis, he entered hospital in March '52 to undergo an operation to alleviate bowel blockage. As a result of complications encountered during the operation, Schellenberg passed away on March 31st. at the age of 42.

As for the man who helped expedite these revised futures, after his posting in Germany, John McCloy went on to head the boards of several major US corporations, as well as advising Presidents from Eisenhower to Reagan. In what can only be described as a continuing penchant for immersing himself in contentious issues, he was later appointed to the Warren Commission, the government panel assigned to investigate the assassination of President John Kennedy. After what had been a lengthy and diverse career, McCloy died in Stamford, Connecticut, on March 11, 1989, three weeks shy of his 94th birthday.

Unlike many of his recently amnestied colleagues, in mid-1952, Höttl had been facing a questionable future. In addition to the troubles created by his 'final' purging by the Americans, a more personal dilemma had surfaced, revolving around the academic future of his second son, Völker. Höttl had faced a similar situation in 1949, when his eldest son, Hagen, was forced to relocate to Vienna in order to complete his education. Hoping to avoid the same scenario with Völker, Höttl had begun to look for ways to resolve the problem.

Völker Höttl 2000

"When my brother was in Vienna attending school he was staying with my grandmother and aunts. It worked out terribly because he could do what he wanted with them and subsequently received bad marks and poor reports. This was the reason my father said that he would try and found a school in the area. He didn't want to have to send his other son to Vienna and repeat it all a second time."

As with the German education system in the 1950's, Austrian students who had completed their first four years of public school were left with three options. Those categorized as low achievers or who wished to end their scholastic endeavours as quickly as possible, were encouraged to attend classes in the Hauptschule. Doing so allowed students to leave the system at the 9th grade, either to learn a craft at a trade school or directly enter the workforce. Those interested in continuing their education but who did not necessarily want to attend university, had the choice of the Realschule, or middle level school. Students here were required to complete the 10th class, and upon graduation could seek entrance to a Berufsschule (trade or technical school) or apply to attend University, albeit with studies limited to certain faculties. The third category was the Gymnasium, the closest equivalent to the University Entrance program offered in North America. To complete this level, it was necessary to attend classes through the 13th grade, at the end of which, one was required to complete a written and oral Abitur, or Matura as it was known in Austria. Once students received their Matura, they were entitled to go on to university, with the only restriction to studies being their grades.

In order to prevent a student's education from being limited by a family's social or economic status, most schools in Austria at the time were financed by the State. Despite that assistance, the possibility of obtaining a Matura in the early '50's was largely restricted to students living in larger urban areas, or those with the financial backing to attend private schools. Prior to 1952, circumstances in Ausseerland dictated that a sizeable majority of students graduating from the Hauptschule moved on to find employment in the Salt Works or other local industry. In what could be viewed as a 'Catch 22', as a result of the limited demand for higher education, authorities deemed the Hauptschule in Bad Aussee sufficient to meet local needs. Anyone interested in furthering their schooling had the option of attending the private Realgymnasium in nearby Bad Goisern, or face the prospect of life in a distant Internat.

Having come from 'a family of limited means', as he often liked to remind his listeners, Höttl had long placed a high degree of importance on academic achievement. Proud of being the sole member amongst his siblings to attain a university education, he wanted to assure such an opportunity was available for his own children. In the summer of 1949, a considerable amount of deliberation took place before it was decided Hagen would be sent to reside with his grandmother and aunts in Vienna. The ten year old began fall classes at a public Vienna Gymnasium, but separated from the strict family environment back home, his grades suffered badly, reaching a climax in the 5th Grade (Grade 10) when he failed to meet the requirements for advancement into the next level.

Völker Höttl 2001:
"With him the studies floundered and his career development turned out to be less stellar than my father had hoped or expected. For a short while he worked in a bank, then for most of his life he was a representative for a pharmaceutical concern. And for my father this was nothing. For him this was a salesman, like every other salesman. I often tried to explain to him that every businessman is a salesman of sorts, right up to the US President, but it was difficult to get him to see this."

Andrea Hofer: 2002
"I often tried to distance myself from my father as a way of avoiding conflict, but Hagen on the other hand was always relenting. ... always relenting. They had a tense relationship."

Disappointed over how Hagen had fared in Vienna, Höttl was adamant about avoiding a repeat performance with Völker. Recognizing that many other people in the community were faced with similar limited options, he began to make discreet inquiries as to how much communal support there might be for the idea of establishing a Realgymnasium in Bad Aussee. With a population base of over 10,000, many of whom had school age children, one might have expected the citizens of Bad Aussee to have welcomed the opportunity to have a Matura school erected within their own district. According to sources however, initial reaction to the plan was far from euphoric. Höttl initially blamed the lack of enthusiasm on the 'provincial mindset', ignoring the possibility the apathy in some circles was not so much with what was being presented, as with who was presenting it. Despite this early reluctance, Höttl was eventually able to attain the support of two prominent Bad Aussee residents, spa physician, Dr. Konrad Hofer, and local bank director, Adolf Pilz. Both men were prepared to back the scheme, not only for the advantages it would provide their own children, but also the substantial economic benefits such an enterprise could bring to the community. A third man reported to have shared that view was Hans Roithner, financial consultant for the Bad Aussee town council. A former school director himself, whose right to teach had been suspended because of his membership in the NSDAP, Roithner, acted as liaison between Höttl and the town administration during the preliminary discussions on the project. Unlike his colleagues however, Roithner would later defer from sending his own son to the very school he helped actualize.

By early fall, negotiations had advanced far enough for Höttl to announce the founding of the *"Mittelschulverein Bad Aussee"*. Naming himself as director and Adolf Pilz as treasurer, he gave notice the official opening of classes would take place on November 6th, 1952. On that day eleven students crowded into a small room above the Lewandowski Bakery in Bad Aussee to begin lessons in History and Geography, taught by the school's sole teacher, Prof. Ernst Schreiner. Despite that rather modest beginning, Höttl was optimistic enough about the school's future to immediately begin plans for expansion. Whether his haste was based on pure confidence or merely a desire to distance himself from a storm building on the horizon was not clear. Considering the reliable track record of his warning radar, it is difficult to imagine Höttl did not have some inkling of what was brewing, even if his ability to alter the circumstances were beyond his control. As a result, barely two months after its launch, circumstances elsewhere brought the exuberance over the school's prospects to a sudden halt.

Early on the morning of January 14th, 1953, Kurt Ponger left his house in Vienna's Soviet sector, intending to drop his daughter off at kindergarten before heading to his office. Presumably unaware of a tail he picked up the moment he crossed into the American sector, he stopped off briefly at the market, before arriving at the school around 8:15am. Shortly after watching his daughter, Lisl enter the building, Ponger's car was approached by three men dressed in civilian clothes. Informed he was under arrest, Ponger was taken into custody by American officials and transported to the city's CIC headquarters. Several minutes earlier in another district of Vienna, a second group of agents had arrested Otto Verber. Held in separate interrogation rooms, both men were informed they were accused of carrying out espionage activities on behalf of the Soviet Union. Later that same day, the pair was put aboard a military aircraft for transport to the States. Within hours of their arrival at a camp outside of Washington D.C. they appeared before Judge Alexander Holtzoff, to hear the official reading of the charges against them. Among the fourteen counts they faced;

- the sale and delivery of lists of American agents to the military intelligence of the Soviet Union.
- the bribing of officers in the American Military Intelligence.
- betraying maps and plans for American manoeuvres.
- recruiting high US officials for intelligence work for the Soviet diplomat, Juri W. Novikow, the second secretary of the Russian Embassy in Washington.
- extensive black market transactions between Austria and West Germany.

No pleas were entered and as neither defendant was able to meet the $50,000 bail, both were remanded in custody for four weeks pending a preliminary hearing.

Back in Austria, news of the arrests swept rapidly through the intelligence community, creating a high degree of anxiety within those sectors linked to either of the two detainees. One of the first to be rounded up for questioning by CIC officials was fellow Austrian and US compatriot, Walter Lauber. Despite having been an intimate business associate of the pair, Lauber was freed after eight days of interrogation in Salzburg. The second figure detained under the broadening dragnet was Berlin-born, US citizen, Ernst Tisloweitz, a good acquaintance of both Ponger and Verber from their days in New York. Unlike Lauber and Tisloweitz, Eva Verber managed to make herself scarce, telling officials she had no knowledge of her husband's illicit activities, before leaving for New York accompanied by her two young children.

By the beginning of February, claims of innocence or ignorance had sprouted amongst most associates of the suspected spies. Amidst this vacuum of relevant testimony, rumours of the pair's purported activities became rife, so much so, a spokesman for the US Commission in Austria was forced to dampen speculation by issuing a statement claiming Ponger had not *"gone over"* to the Soviets while working at Nuremberg in 1945. It wasn't long before the reverberations of the developing scandal reached Alt Aussee. Aware his own connection to Ponger was bound to be detected in the ensuing investigation, Höttl began a letter campaign designed to emphasize the harmlessness of their affiliation. Writing to his friend and colleague, Baron Heinrich (Harry) Mast, Höttl spelled out his concern about *'wrongly'* being drawn into the fray.

Höttl: Jan. 16, 1953

"Dear Harry:

What do you say about the odd espionage affair in Vienna? The oddest thing about it is that I have actually known these people for years so I must therefore be a Soviet agent. Joking aside, I still can't understand. why these people never approached me? If they had been smart they would certainly have been able to approach me from some direction. It really is quite obscure to me... If the Russian Intelligence Service is not more competent than this then I should be very happy. In any case I am puzzled that I never noticed anything about them which was indicative. I certainly hope that I won't get drawn into this matter because there would be a good deal of fun for certain people. In any case it would be a good thing if my correspondence were discovered, since it makes it clear that I dealt with these people only concerning photographs and concerning the arrangement of export licenses. Please give me your advice on this whole matter, particularly as to what I should do now. Is there any point in my reporting now what I know? I certainly know of nothing of professional interest. On the other hand, I would certainly like to assist in clearing up the case if the people are really guilty. A certain feeling of revenge exists here on my part because I was taken in. In total, this is a very strange matter".

The none too subtle attempt to divert suspicion was repeated in a second letter that same day, this one directed to a man Höttl claimed to have met through Ponger. Unlike Mast however, venturing to use Theodor von Albert to underscore his innocence involved considerable risk. Von Albert and his partner, Armand Fellner were jointly responsible for the publication of a journal called Interreport Ost. Founded in 1950 and distributed by Ponger's Central European Press and Literary Agency, the magazine was widely known in intelligence circles and generally viewed as a cover for the collection of intelligence destined for the French, Israeli and Austrian Intelligence Services.

Höttl: Jan. 16th, 1953

"Dear Theo:

What do you say about the new espionage case in Vienna? An odd story. As you already know, I know these brothers and considered it out of the question that they could be Soviet agents. I should be most interested to know what is at the bottom of the case. Why, for example did these people never make any attempt to recruit me? I can only explain it to myself by supposing that it was clear to them that because of my clear idealogical orientation nothing was to be gained. But on the other hand, they may have attempted to make some sort of play in order to learn my connections. I had really trusted them since I could not believe that OSS officers could be Soviet agents. It is a point against their professional competence if the whole story is true. In any case I will be thankful to Angerer for any information and will take a personal interest in it. If Angerer, has any special questions, I am at his disposal but I would prefer not to be named as a source, since I do not particularly wish to be known as an acquaintance of such people."

The man Höttl was referring to was Johann Angerer, a member of the Salzburg police, and reputedly a sub-agent of von Albert's. Having sensed a direct approach to Angerer might raise suspicions, Höttl had concluded the best method of learning how much the other side knew about Ponger's alleged black market activities, was to go through von Albert. Noticeably irritated at having the subject broached in an open letter, von Albert responded within twenty-four hours.

Theo von Albert: Jan. 17th. 1953
"Dear Willi:
The story about Kurt Ponger is not most amusing. The arrest occurred in part because of certain information which was gathered by Angerer, partly through me and partly through you. Therefore our further conversation had best be oral. I request to know everything that you know about the case because I shall certainly learn a good deal more myself."

As it was, Höttl had been sharing von Albert's correspondence with Mast, who logged back on two days later with his own perception of events.

Mast: Jan. 19th, 1953
"Dear Willi:
To get started right away on the Ponger case. In this matter I have the feeling that it is not wise to act prematurely. Especially since, if they have found the correspondence, which I would approve of, the basic harmlessness of the affair is clear. The main question in any event, is how you came to know those people. Either this question is clear from the correspondence or you have some other plausible explanation. More unpleasant is the affair in Salzburg, since it is not known whence the good Angerer got those names and whether our friends in Gmunden B, know more or knew more about this case. If so, then enormous falsehoods could be perpetrated."

Both Höttl and Mast had reason to be concerned about the Salzburg affair, which centred on alleged CIC involvement in black market activities. Such operations had become prevalent ever since US troops who fought in Germany and Austria, had been replaced by US occupation forces. Not having personally experienced the horrors of the concentration camps, these new men held a different attitude towards dealing with the Germans and Austrians. The fact various customs officials on both the Austrian/German border and in Munich participated in the black market schemes, made it easier for all to become involved, with most thinking the risks of detection relatively low. Although American officials had known for sometime that Ponger and Verber were transporting non-taxed luxury articles, like coffee and cigarettes, across the frontier in vehicles equipped with identification documents from CIC Salzburg headquarters, they had refrained from taking any action for fear of jeopardizing an on-going investigation into what they suspected was their espionage for the Soviets. Although Höttl and Mast were suspected of having dabbled in the black market activities, it wasn't so much the fear of becoming entangled in that growing scandal which made them nervous, but rather a fear their involvement in other activities might be exposed.

Eager to know more about the status of the investigation, Mast suggested that former SS Major Karl Hass, Höttl's former deputy in Italy, be given the mission of obtaining more information. As a agent of the CIC as well as the Gehlen Organization, Hass could likely have acquired such information had Mast not abandoned the plan after getting wind of how events in Washington were unfolding.

Mast: Jan. 22nd. 1953
"Dear Willi:
Internal events have occurred which have postponed the urgency of this matter, since now, as is apparent from the newspapers, the prosecution has formally indicted the two defendants and the trial is scheduled to begin on March 3rd. From the European point of view this would mean that the investigation has been concluded. In any case, however, I still hold to my opinion, that for the time being, you should do nothing."

Höttl did not agree that doing nothing was the best way to proceed, but pressing obligations of running the school helped convince him to accept Mast's counsel for the time being. Just when it seemed the intrigue couldn't get any more impenetrable, Höttl wrote again to Mast, assuring him matters were under control and that an alternative plan was already in the works.

Höttl: Jan. 23rd. 1953
"Dear Harry:
Many thanks for your fine communication of the 19th of January. In the case of P.(Ponger), I agree with you completely and certainly do not wish to inform any of A's (Angerer) people as long as the investigation is still in progress. However, I have discovered a good solution. In a completely private and personal copy, I have informed my Schneider friend of this matter. He asked me to give him a complete written report concerning my acquaintance, which would be held until I specifically gave him the permission to use it. If I should get into any sort of difficulties, I could therefore state at any time that I had

given my information to a reputable firm. The connection of my Schneider friend in the affair is very interesting, although I naturally do not know whether it is purely personal or professional. He was not an intimate of Ponger,... but also believes that there is something peculiar in the case. The situation does not ring true. I am extremely curious to find out what will come of the case. Any further information that I have on it, I will give to you orally."

The 'Schneider' friend Höttl mentioned was Rupert Mandl, a close associate from their days at SD regional headquarters in Vienna. Like so many former colleagues, Mandl had not had gone wanting for a job after the war, hired on to apply his extensive intelligence experience with the Gehlen Organization. Hoping limited admissions might forestall a broader investigation, Höttl had prepared a report for Mandl in which he described his connections to Ponger and Verber. The latter was depicted as a clever, witty, and practical person, but definitely the junior partner of the pair. Ponger was presented as a nationally minded individual who viewed himself more a Jew than an American. In the report Höttl admitted having been in regular communication with Ponger from 1948 to October 1952, explaining how the earlier contact had revolved around the purchase of CEPLA owned photos for his various articles. Their association had only intensified, Höttl maintained, after Ponger landed a contract with a Swiss publishing firm for the publication of 'The Secret Front'. Contending that Ponger had always handled him in a fair and humane manner, Höttl was much less flattering when it came to commenting on Vera Ponger. Conceding he had only met her once, he was convinced the *"clever and self-assured"* woman had worn the pants in the family, and likely called the shots in any intelligence activities the pair might have been involved in. Having jettisoned any feigned claims of bewilderment at not having been approached for intelligence, Höttl did reveal that Ponger had expressed interest in learning more about Gestapo chief Heinrich Müller and Adolf Eichmann, during one of his visits to Alt Aussee. Admitting he had initially presumed Ponger's interest in Eichmann had been sparked by the $100,000 bounty on the fugitive's head, Höttl claimed he later felt it may have stemmed from Ponger's allegedly having worked for Israeli intelligence in Vienna.

Within days of submitting the report to Mandl, Höttl was visited by CIC agents, wishing to question him on statements made in the document. Unsettled by the encounter, two days later, Höttl found it prudent to deliver a 12 page document to CIC investigating officer Rolf E. Ringer, in which his dealings with Ponger and Verber were laid out in much greater detail. As he had done with his correspondence with Mandl, he again strove to emphasize his role as an unwitting victim with no knowledge of schemes to penetrate the security apparatus of US forces in Austria.

Meanwhile in Washington, prosecutors had managed to circumvent the slow pace of justice to assure the preliminary hearing scheduled for March began on time. Despite the sobering prospect of lengthy prison terms upon conviction, neither the 39 year old Ponger, nor his 31 year old accomplice showed a willingness to co-operate with the court. Both entered pleas of *"not guilty"* and were remanded over for trial set to begin on April 20th.

Following the visit by CIC authorities, Höttl tried to keep abreast of the dispensation of justice in Washington as best he could. With each passing day producing no visible action against him, his guarded optimism gradually began to take on an element of smugness. It was after all not the first time he'd been under suspicion for maintaining ties to Soviet operatives. Whereas in the past such contacts had been rationalized with the argument they were an integral part of his intelligence work, once beyond the direct control of CIC officials following his dismissal, Höttl had had a free hand to expand his eastern ties with relative impunity. Somewhat ironically, his access to those people had often been expedited by organizations like OG, which although ostensibly mandated to prevent Soviet spies from infiltrating Western Europe, had in fact itself become riddled with them. The same was true to a lesser extent with the CIC, which by accepting compromised Nazis into its ranks, had made itself vulnerable to those agents being blackmailed. Unlike their American counterparts who tended to overlook a compromised past if it served their purposes, Soviet officials often used incriminating material in their possession to 'coax' former Nazis into serving as double agents.

Still hoping to expose the extent of Höttl's involvement in the Ponger/ Verber imbroglio but aware the evidence linking him to Communist operatives and sympathizers was thin, investigators decided to employ other methods that could help to increase the odds of securing an indictment. On March 25th, CIC agent Rolf E. Ringer arrived in the Austrian town of Bad Ischl for a pre-arranged meeting with Höttl. At some point in their discussions, Ringer requested Höttl accompany him back to Salzburg for further talks. Feigned or not, Höttl showed no cause for concern and agreed. Upon arrival however, he was taken to a building at Hellbrunnerstr. 5, and subjected to several hours of intense questioning concerning his relationship with Ponger and Verber. When the session ended, he was shown a warrant for his arrest on suspicion of being a Soviet double agent. A second interrogation followed that afternoon and it was after six in the evening before Höttl was transferred to 'comfortable quarters' meant to serve as a temporary cell. Despite his tendency to slip into bravado, Höttl knew that current investigators had access to more information than had been the case in Berlin, Freising or Nuremberg. What he didn't know however, was that his uncertainty was matched by investigators, who after the first round of questioning, had realized how difficult it would be to tie him to the American spies.

Simultaneous to events in Salzburg, a contingent of American soldiers arrived in Alt Aussee to carry out a court-sanctioned search of Hottl's home and office. Working throughout the afternoon and evening, their efforts netted over 20,000 documents, all of which were packed up and carted off to Salzburg. The fact the material was so accessible caused some investigators to suspect much of it may have been planted, with more incriminating material having already been destroyed or hidden. Their curiosity piqued by the activities taking place at Höttl's residence, locals saw to it that news of his 'problems' spread quickly.

Aware of the pressure the arrest of an Austrian citizen could bring to bear, American authorities felt obligated to issue a number of press releases explaining that Höttl was being held after having been linked to an operation to supply US intelligence to the Soviets. In addition to indicating the arrest was warranted, officials hoped the adverse publicity would help discredit Höttl amongst other intelligence services once and for all.

On the afternoon of March 28th, a third round of interrogation began, running straight through to the late evening. Initial questioning pretty much followed the line of the first two sessions, but at some point, patience over Höttl's restrained co-operation became exhausted. As part of a plan to encourage him to be more forthcoming, the next morning he was awakened and placed in solitary confinement in much less agreeable surroundings. Provided a typewriter and paper, he was instructed to supply all the information relevant to the case, and warned the isolation would remain in force until he chose to abandon his previous tactics. Before leaving him to the task, Höttl was informed he would undergo a polygraph test at the next session. Several hours later, he was ushered into the interrogation room and hooked up to the machine. Much to the disappointment of investigators however, rather than monitoring increased tension to relevant questions, the strongest responses were registered in instances where investigators were certain he was not lying. Unbeknownst to investigators, a combination of low blood pressure and a circulatory defect, was causing the machine to register a general level of tension in Höttl's breathing, rendering the changes in his pulse rate virtually meaningless. With no way of accurately assessing answers to important questions, such as whether he had concealed or destroyed documents related to the case, investigators were forced to abandon the procedure and return Höttl to his cell. In spite of the polygraph's flawed data, authorities had observed a slight change in Höttl's demeanour during the test. Convinced he was concealing information, they decided to extend his solitary confinement indefinitely in the hope it would produce a more co-operative attitude. By April 3rd the strategy started to have its desired effect as Höttl ventured beyond his previous borders to offer a number of explanations.

While that was going on, officials elsewhere were busy sifting through the massive cache of documents confiscated at Höttl's home. Amongst the items found in the raid were a Liechtenstein passport in the name of Hans Eberhard Mayer, a 7.65 mm Walther PPK Automatic pistol, five blank Austrian identity cards, and 1,495 counterfeit English ten pound notes. Once pertinent sections of the voluminous files had been screened, documented and photographed, summarized reports were forwarded on to investigators. Compiled primarily by CIC agent Arthur J. Stone, the transcripts enabled Salzburg investigators to compare relevant sections with information from the interrogations. Besides the letters Höttl and Ponger had exchanged, of most significance was a list of prospective agents for an envisioned network he had planned to establish following his dismissal from the CIC, a list that bore many of the same names now linked to the Ponger-Verber affair.

In what was clearly part of a strategy to avoid guilt by association, Höttl attempted to crowd the stage with players he claimed had held much stronger ties to Ponger than himself. Of the seventy-five individuals named since the eruption of the scandal, albeit not all from Höttl, many were already known quantities within the CIC's domain. One of the first to appear on the radar was former SS Oberführer, Wilhelm Krichbaum. Born May 7th 1896, in Wiesbaden, Krichbaum was an early Nazi supporter, a stance he was rewarded for with appointment as chief deputy to Gestapo leader, Heinrich Müller, following Hitler's ascension to power. In an accompanying role as head of the German Army's much feared Secret Military Police, Krichbaum was linked to numerous criminal activities attributed to that organization during the war. Like so many, he was not held accountable for those alleged crimes but instead managed to find his way on to the US payroll, serving first with the CIC, and then the Gehlen Organization, where as a district chief, he was responsible for recruiting other former Nazis into the agency.

Höttl claimed Krichbaum and Ponger had held a number of clandestine meetings together, prompting investigators in Salzburg to haul the former in for questioning. Confronted with allegations the meetings had involved intelligence matters, Krichbaum maintained a qualified silence, not only to protect himself from possible incrimination, but also to avoid exposing his ties to someone even more dubious than himself.

Born in Dresden on March 18th, 1918, Heinz Felfe worked in the RSHA during the war, supplying personal protection for many high ranking officials in the Nazi regime. He later moved to Schellenberg's Amt VI, serving as the SD Referat for Switzerland from 1943 until the close of the war. Captured by the British in 1945, Felfe obtained his release in 1946 by reportedly agreeing to work for British Intelligence. Unbeknownst to his British handlers however, he had also been successfully recruited by the Soviets while stationed in Münster in northern Germany. Not satisfied with merely being a double agent, in November 1951, Felfe joined the ranks of the Gehlen Organization, going on to become a senior officer in an unit dealing with counter-espionage against the Soviet Union. Felfe was apparently very good at his craft, as evidenced by the fact a decade would pass before he was exposed as a KGB mole within OG's successor, the Bundesnachrichtendienst (BND). Sentenced to 14 years in 1963, he was released in 1969 as part of a spy exchange with East Germany.

In regards to Krichbaum, intelligence officials in Salzburg were unable to obtain any relevant information from him. That did not prevent them from keeping tabs on his activities up until 1961. Caught up in the aftermath of another scandal at that time, he was arrested, tried and convicted of having been a long-term Soviet agent. A subsequent re-appraisal of his postwar allegiances compiled by the CIA in 1963, implied Krichbaum had likely begun working for the Soviets as early as 1950.

Rounding off the triumvirate of agents purportedly within Ponger's alleged inner circle was former SS Major Josef Adolf Urban. A former 'trusted agent' of Amt VI, who at one time was also the Referat for Hungary, after the war Urban was involved in intelligence activities with a variety of agencies, thought to have included the Americans, British, French and Israelis. Although mention of Krichbaum, Felfe and Urban did serve to temporarily shift some of the focus away from Höttl, his insinuations about the trio were called into question when it was revealed he and Urban had recently had a falling out, sufficient motivation for wanting to discredit an erstwhile colleague.

Still hoping to refute or corroborate Höttl's claimed relationship with Ponger and Verber, authorities visited the Salzburg residence of Theo von Albert on April 1st. In what they described was more a conversation than an interrogation, von Albert traced the history of his contact with Höttl, starting with visits the latter had made to his Salzburg apartment, ostensibly seeking material for an upcoming book. According to von Albert's recollections, it was after several visits that Höttl admitted he was in fact gathering political and economic information about southeastern European countries for a West German intelligence agency. He then went on to boast of his excellent contacts to Allen Dulles and Col. Bill Donovan of the OSS, identifying himself as the Austrian representative of Amt Blank, before asking whether von Albert would be interested in assisting him in his endeavours. A brief round of negotiations followed, ending with the offer of a monthly fee of 1500 Austrian Schillings, and the promise to help von Albert develop contacts with West German newspapers. Von Albert told investigators that once he had agreed to the offer, communication between them from that point on had assumed the form of written reports, forwarded to Höttl in Linz via Harry Mast. The information in the reports reportedly came from confidential east European contacts, von Albert claimed he was not at liberty to reveal. The arrangement had continued until the fall of 1952, at which time he was approached by two Amt Blank colleagues who informed him Höttl was no longer with the agency. Von Albert's subsequent decision to severe his ties with Höttl, was also influenced by the discovery that much of the information he had been supplying to him, was finding its way into the hands of other agencies, including the Austrian State Police and Austrian Interior Ministry.

As officials continued to run into a series of dead ends, prospects for keeping Höttl in custody began to dwindle. In another effort to break the impasse, they chose to suspend his isolation and subject him to another round of interrogations. Tired of his belaboured image of somehow having been the sole member of Ponger's circle not to have cultivated Soviet links, investigators demanded to know how Höttl could have remained oblivious to the subterfuge swirling around him. Aware that investigators had begun to cover the same ground over and over, backed by the fact no official charges had been laid against him, Höttl sensed the momentum was shifting in his favour. Hoping to call what he perceived as a continuing bluff, he adopted a more sanguine manner, claiming his enduring ignorance was simply the result of his unfamiliarity with espionage techniques at the collection level, insinuating he had been too busy with overseeing operations to have taken notice or responsibility for the activities of individual colleagues. Ratcheting up the pressure, he then threatened to retract all of his previous testimony, slyly warning of his ability to publicly divulge certain information on American intelligence activities and policies that could prove highly embarrassing to the agency.

A Höttl 'acquaintance': 1960
"*A civil servant is sloppy with the finances. The story is covered up but someone hears about it and makes a note of it for future use. A man gets involved with corruption, has a little taste from bribes, or perhaps he has a friend on the side. A respectable politician has an affair. Everything comes into the files. This isn't extortion. It could come to extortion when someone was dumb enough to provoke the collector. But nobody is that dumb... Höttl is the type of man who keeps files.*"

Although Höttl did not specify a deadline to act, his threats prompted authorities to review their case against him. Faced with the reality there was not enough evidence to put him where they felt he belonged, investigators concluded the best alternative was to do everything in their power to emasculate him as a functioning force within the entire intelligence community. Believing such a move would effectively end his days as an operative and render him incapable of further harassing former, current or future clients, they saw to it that copies of Stone's reports were widely distributed amongst their brethren. Although the tactic did manage to provide temporary solace, it could do little to prevent the inevitable, and on April 11th, officials watched as Höttl once again walked back into freedom.

Less than two weeks after Höttl left the confines of his Salzburg cell for the final time, the wheels of justice in Washington entered a crucial phase. Since the beginning of Ponger and Verber's trial, prosecutors had struggled with the unenviable task of trying to establish the defendants' guilt without revealing sensitive elements of the US intelligence service. They were also dealing with a series of persistent rumours, one of which implied both men had originally been *"sent in"* by US Military officials to de-brief selected refugees streaming in from eastern bloc countries, only to turn on their backs on their benefactors and become double agents. A second rumour portrayed them as having been part of an operation designed to locate and entrap Soviet moles within American intelligence circles. In either case, as the theories went, once exposed, the pair were destined to be sacrificed so that America's pragmatic policies could be preserved.

In a classic example of the left hand keeping the right hand from knowing what it was doing, court proceedings were conducted behind closed doors under the jurisdiction of Judge Alexander Holtzoff. The secrecy would extend beyond the trial, with transcripts and all accompanying evidence designated as *"classified"* material, and consigned to the vaults of the National Archives in perpetuity. Portions of that intentional fog however, were lifted in 2003, when a number of files documenting America's intelligence activities in post-war Europe were de-classified under the Freedom of Information Act. Amongst the documents released was a top secret FBI memo written in June of 1957, that implied there had been a lot more to the Ponger/Verber case than American officials were interested in disclosing. One of the most telling features of the memorandum was something not included in it, namely CEPLA. Despite having been tagged as Ponger's cover for returning to Vienna, there was little mention of the company during the trial. Aware of his ties to the firm, prosecutors chose not to delve into its origins or how salaries could regularly be drawn from a company that never showed any profits. The lack of interest in CEPLA continued to feed speculation the company had been a CIC front, established to carry out the kind of activities Ponger and Verber were now accused of participating in.

From the evidence at their disposal in 1953, investigators suspected Ponger had been recruited by Soviet agents not long after his arrival in Vienna. They also believed he had recruited his brother-in-law into the Soviet fold shortly thereafter, urging him to approach an employee of the US forces stationed in Austria, whose acquaintance he had made at Nuremberg. With access to sensitive military intelligence data, 'Mr. Z' was precisely the type of *'insider'* Ponger was looking for. Although initially reticent to join the operation, 'Mr. Z' ultimately agreed to participate and for the next year and a half regularly performed the tasks asked of him. In January 1951 however, he was unexpectedly transferred back to Washington, forcing Ponger and Verber to scramble for alternative arrangements. Verber enrolled at the University of Vienna and began a search for new potential informants among the various military personnel studying there under the GI Bill. Parallel to that recruitment drive, which was already under CIC surveillance, officials requested that colleagues in Washington place *"Mr.Z"* under observation to determine whether he was continuing to work for Ponger and Verber from his new station. Supplemented by the surveillance in Vienna, the monitoring in Washington eventually paid off, leading to the exposure of a Russian diplomat named Yuri V. Novikov as a co-conspirator in Ponger's operation.

Amongst the 2000 top secret documents seized at the time of Novikov's detainment, was a brief report detailing what Ponger and Verber had reportedly handed over to the Soviets, which included;

- plans for American manoeuvres and lists of agents in the American intelligence service.
- data on US Air Force Personnel stationed abroad,
- the morale of USFA officers and enlisted personnel.
- USFA interrogation techniques.
- the identity of US intelligence sources.
- the names of US military personnel destined for overseas service, and files containing documentation of Russian installations and military capacities.

As if untangling the threads of the case wasn't already difficult enough, an FBI report released in 1957 depicted the pair as having become double agents in order to supply the Soviets with a high proportion of disinformation. According to this report, Mr. "Z" 's entry had merely been an insurance policy to assure Ponger and Verber stayed within the rules of the complicated game.

If true, there was no explanation as to why it took the better part of two and a half years for the collected evidence to translate into a series of arrests.

In any event, once confronted with the material amassed against them, both Ponger and Verber changed their pleas to guilty. From that point, jurisprudence needed less than 50 days to reach a verdict. Convicted of conspiring to commit espionage, Ponger was sentenced on June 15th, to serve between 5 and 15 years at the federal penitentiary in Atlanta, Georgia. That same day, Verber was given three to ten years, to be served in the State Prison in Pennsylvania.

In the aftermath of the affair, the consensus amongst most analysts was that the Americans had been duped by their own people, not terribly surprising considering their previous affiliation with Communist groups. The fact that justice was carried out away from prying eyes was seen as another indication officials within the intelligence hierarchy had been unable to exercise adequate control over their own creations. Another clue to a possible cover-up were the sentences themselves. Conspiracy to commit espionage qualified as treason in most books, a crime normally dealt with much more severely. The leniency shown seemed to imply that in exchange for a lighter sentence, lips would remain sealed. As for the scandal's impact on the families and CEPLA associates, three board members, including Vera Ponger, resigned their posts in May 1953. The company remained in limbo until October when an application was made to the State of New York for its official dissolution. Vera Ponger remained in Vienna following her husband's arrest, but did not live to see his release, passing away in 1957. Eva Verber, having already made a hasty retreat to New York, remained in the shadows, shielding her children from the publicity surrounding the trial and verdicts. At some point during his incarceration, she filed for divorce, re-married and moved to California.

After serving out their respective terms, ten years for Ponger, and seven for Verber, both men returned to Austria. Made stateless by his espionage conviction, in 1962 Ponger was forced to fight to regain the Austrian citizenship he had surrendered in the 1940's. Drifting through a series of odd jobs, he eventually landed back in the world of publishing, working as a journalist for several Communist newspapers, until passing away on July 30th, 1979. Upon his return, Verber studied accountancy, becoming a CPA and starting a business with another partner. Obligated to work past the normal age of retirement, he was on a business trip to Moscow in 1994, when he suffered the first of two heart attacks. Despite receiving treatment at a local hospital, he died there on July 21st, at the age of 73.

Whether either ever had any contact with Höttl again is uncertain. No doubt grateful he had survived the scandal relatively unscathed, Höttl refrained from acknowledging the pair in any of his subsequent musings. Asked about his former associates in an 1999 interview, Höttl's response was selective amnesia at its best.

Höttl: 1999

"I had been friends with Ponger and his partner Otto Verber. They had both been CIC officers and were both Jewish. They met me here in Alt Aussee, they were in Alt Aussee and had an apartment here and they often visited me. We were...well friends is an exaggeration, but we were good acquaintances. Also with my wife. They were both Viennese Jews who could speak the old Viennese, so that made it easier to speak with them... They weren't convicted, but suspected of being Soviet spies. In any case one day, CIC officers arrested me here and took me to Salzburg. I was locked in a cellar and it was awhile before I could come out... and until I was released, I was accused of being an undetected Russian agent. They thought, well if they've been by Höttl, then he is one too."

As a footnote to the entire saga, in December 1963, an exposed Russian spy with the code name Adelade, made the claim Höttl had indeed once been a highly paid Soviet agent. But with no other details linking him to the dismantled spy ring, Adelade and his allegations simply slid back into the swamp of reputed history.

Völker Höttl: 2000

"I can still recall this today, because I was on my way home from school that afternoon and they were hauling away all his files. They took everything with them. And they took him to Glasenbach by Salzburg. And then they took his secretary as well. I can't remember anymore how long they held them but I'd estimate 3 weeks. It must have been about 3 weeks. But then after all of this had taken place, the time with all the contacts was finished. It was over for both sides, … nobody trusted him anymore."

The recent events in Salzburg had once again made Höttl the focus of gossip at local cafes and *"Stammtische"*. Chastened by the experience, he attempted to put the entire escapade behind him by re-immersing himself in the daily obligations of running the school. One of the problems requiring particular attention was the on-going struggle to procure the *"Öffentliche Recht"* (ÖR), basically the right to conduct final examinations and issue the much sought after Matura. Aware from the start that its acquisition was essential to the school's future, Höttl had initiated steps to procure it shortly after the school's inauguration in 1952. Since doing so, he had been met by a series of what he viewed as foot-dragging tactics by education officials in Vienna.

Parallel to that unresolved issue was the need for expansion. In order to alleviate the problems an increased staff and student population were causing, Höttl and his associates had begun to explore the possibilities of renting or leasing a number of supplementary buildings in the area. As was the case with many stages of the school's development, sources of funding for the planned expansion carried their share of controversy. In later years, Höttl would claim royalties from overseas sales of 'The Secret Front' had been used as collateral for the needed loans. That may have covered a portion of the expected costs, but the bulk of the monies came from a deal worked out between the town council, school administrators and the parents association, which was rumoured to have made several large donations to the cause itself. Handled through the local bank director, Adolf Pilz, and the town council's liaison, Dr. Hans Roithner, who in the interim had become Höttl's deputy director at the school, the deal authorized the purchase of several auxiliary buildings to meet the expected demands, receipt of the Öffentliche Recht would generate. A proviso in the agreement made the loan dependant on Höttl's agreeing to incorporate the school into what would ultimately become the Private Middle School Gmbh. Bad Aussee.

The royalties and bank loan had not been the only source of support for expansion. One mysterious benefactor was reported to have been a former SS Captain by the name of Dr. Hermann Oberascher. According to an article in the Austrian newspaper, Volksstimme on May 5th, 1961, Oberascher and his wife, Theresia Patorek, both of whom were listed as residents of Iran, allegedly owned one quarter of the assets of the newly incorporated company. Other than his having been an SS staff doctor, little is known about Oberascher's activities during the war, other than he felt compelled to head to the relative safety of Persia shortly before Germany's defeat. Once there, the Salzburg native reportedly re-established himself with the help of funds deposited there by underground Nazi agents. Over time he was able to build up a profitable practice with a patient clientele that allegedly included Shah Rezi Pahlevi. What would prompt a successful doctor and his wife to invest as silent partners in a small provincial school in Austria, was puzzling, especially given there is no record of either ever having visited the school or shown any interest in its day to day running.

Whatever the origins of the funding, the first structure acquired was a stately old building at Obertressen 66, located in the Bad Aussee section of Praunfalk. Prone to waxing fondly whenever recalling *"his villa"*, Höttl was noticeably less effusive when it came to explaining how it became available. Nestled in the hills above the town, Villa Margit, had once belonged to a Jewish lawyer named Weisshut. Following its *'Aryanization'* in the late 1930's, the building had stood empty for a number of years. Still unclaimed after the war, it was transferred to the jurisdiction of the Bad Aussee town council in the mid 1950's. Rumoured to have been eager to part with it, mainly because of the extensive renovations required, council members managed to conclude a purchase agreement with Höttl's group in April 1956. Not only did the acquisition of Villa Margit help to stabilize the school's position in the community, it also spurred the Ministry of Education in Vienna to finally reach a decision regarding the 'Öffentliche Recht.' Although no official explanation was ever given for the three year impasse, many believe the delay had been tied to Höttl's past and as well as his repeated *'encounters'* with the Americans.

With the Ministry's official granting of the OR on June 6th, 1956, students previously forced to write their final exams either at the Gymnasium in nearby Bad Goisern, or be accompanied to Vienna by Elfriede Höttl, to write before the Proofing Commission of the city's School Board, now had the right to sit for their Matura exams on home turf.

Höttl: 1999

"The responsibility of a historian is normally to portray the history of his country, for his country, ... to answer questions that may arise concerning that history. The historian should first assess whether information is true or not, assure that the source is a serious one. Then one can write or discuss it. ... when one was an intelligence officer himself, one can better evaluate whether or not something is true."

In spite of his habit of anointing himself a 'respected historian', Höttl's motives for preserving the facts were not always as laudable as he intimated. Having already benefitted from the sums produced by the publication of 'The Secret Front', he continued to be driven by the financial prospects of catering to a burgeoning public demand for details on the inner-workings of the Third Reich. In line with that goal, shortly after his return from Salzburg, he began the task of sifting through his sizeable reservoir of exploits for a suitable subject to write about. One of the factors affecting Höttl's decision to portray the people and events of Operation Bernhard, was the response that had been engendered by an earlier publication entitled 'Wunderwaffe Falschgeld'(Counterfeit Money:The Wonder Weapon). Published in Switzerland in 1952, the book had sold well, in part because of the '*exclusive*' facts provided by a man named Dr. Ostermann. Although Höttl would later deny having had any association with Ostermann, many of the same '*facts*' to grace the Swiss book, would find their way onto the pages of his own epic. What ultimately set Höttl's book apart was that its author had actually partaken in a counterfeiting operation during the course of a war. Acknowledging such involvement openly however, would have been tantamount to confessing to a criminal act. In order to avoid such a scenario, Höttl reached a secret accord with his publisher, Welsermühl, Wels & Starnberg, guaranteeing that publication would only take place once the ten year Statute of Limitations on possible prosecution had expired.

Despite the precautions taken to allow him to elaborate, which once again included using the pseudonym, Walter Hagen, Höttl still proved incapable of delivering a completely honest accounting. Authenticity however, was apparently not of major concern to numerous publications in Austria and Germany, which in their rush to print excerpts of 'Unternehmen

Bernhard', showed surprising disregard for the common practice of confirming facts. A closer scrutiny of Höttl's recollections only began when a Viennese bookbinder who had been in charge of paper testing at Sachsenhausen, read a review of the book in a German magazine. Incensed at the glaring misrepresentation he and his fellow workers had received at Höttl's hands, Hans Kurzweil wrote to the magazine's editors demanding a retraction. When the publication refused, Kurzweil initiated libel suits against both Höttl and the magazine in Germany and Austria. The heart of Kurzweil's case centred on statements that implied concentration camp inmates participating in OB, had previously been part of the criminal elite in Germany.

Höttl: 1955 (Excerpt from OB)

"Krüger had gathered convicted counterfeiters together from assorted concentration camps, who before the war had been held in "security custody". He also used professional criminals as the original participants fell away. Thus did OB operation come to be more and more under the hands of professional counterfeiters".

In his petition, Kurzweil asserted that almost all prisoners selected to work in Operation Bernhard had been printers, engravers, and bank officials in their civilian careers. The singular exception was Salomon Smolianoff, a professional counterfeiter, who had worked as a re-touch specialist in the forging of American dollars. Höttl's fabrication, Kurzweil argued, was nothing more than a bald attempt to distort the SD's role in helping to organize the scheme. After what first appeared destined to be *"Aussage gegen Aussage"*, the case took a surprising twist in August 1956, when an unsolicited affidavit from no less than Bernhard Krüger himself, was presented to the Bonn court. Fiercely contesting Höttl's allusions, the former head of Operation Bernhard confirmed Kurzweil's claim that only one man in the operation had held a criminal record.

The second of Höttl's inventions to be contested was the awarding of medals. Höttl had claimed that as a consequence of the operation's overwhelming success, Krüger had approached Amt VI chief Walter Schellenberg to recommend that twelve of OB's prison workers be awarded medals for their service. According to Höttl, Schellenberg had chosen to ignore the request, prompting Krüger to turn to him for assistance in pursuing the idea. Claiming to have by-passed the overly cautious Schellenberg, Höttl purported to have gained the direct support of Kaltenbrunner's adjutant, Arthur Scheidler, who in turn merely slipped the request into a pile of daily reports Kaltenbrunner often initialed without reading. According to Höttl's version of events, in October 1943, the Commandant of the Sachsenhausen camp had discovered several prisoners in possession of medals and ordered an immediate investigation.

Höttl: 1955 (Excerpt from OB)

"Kaltenbrunner fortunately possessed a sense of humour....He called me and cynically congratulated me on having succeeded on being the first to award a War Service medal to a Jew. I suffered no repercussions, and it was actually three recipients who were Jews."

As flippant as Höttl's recollection of the episode had been, it was nonetheless another indication of the relationship he had held with Kaltenbrunner. Not many Reich officials would have been excused with such a reprimand under similar circumstances.

A third excerpt Kurzweil took issue with was Höttl's claim that none of the prisoners involved in OB had met a violent end. Presented with the countering testimony of numerous survivors from OB's ranks, courts in Austria and Germany ultimately ruled in Kurzweil's favour on all accounts. For some reason however, only Austrian officials saw fit to demand a public retraction. Although Höttl did submit to the court order, he did so without a tinge of regret. Another five years would pass before he was willing to offer a rational explanation for having taken such liberty with the truth.

Höttl: 1961

"In contrast to my previous work, (The Secret Front) which was grounded in 'historical accuracy', OB is to a great extent, a work of journalism, comparable to the so called true accounts that are so prevalent today."

Former OB workers were not the only ones swept into the spotlight by Höttl's 'accounting' of the operation. Others named in the excerpts, who had established lucrative post-war businesses in the interim, were less than pleased with the attention their former colleague's musings had unleashed. Sensing their reputations might be threatened by the revelations, several chose to instigate libel charges. As a result, on March 7th 1956, Höttl received notice to attend the State Court in Munich to answer accusations of having published a number of *"falsehoods"* in 'Unternehmen Bernhard'. The case, which some observers later labelled 'a mud-slinging match amongst bandits', pitted Höttl against former OB agent Georg Spencer Spitz. Reputed to have previously been a Vienna-based banker, Spitz had reportedly later used his talents to thrive in the unfettered world of counterfeiting, eventually becoming OB's top distributor for Holland, Belgium and northern France. Unlike many of his former colleagues, whose influence notably diminished after the war, Spitz was able to apply his considerable skills to re-establish himself in banking, using what some sources suspected were OB resources to invest in a number of legitimate businesses. By the early 1950's his influence within German business circles had reached a point where he was considered one of Germany's 'upstanding citizens'. Not long after hearing of the book's impending publication, Spitz had used some of his contacts to obtain a galley proof. Greatly perturbed by what he read, he immediately contacted Höttl, offering to buy out the entire first edition if Höttl agreed to remove the offending pages from future editions. Höttl's refusal is believed to have been the provocation for Spitz's subsequent lawsuit. After several months studying the evidence, a Munich court ruled in favour of the plaintiff, ordering the 12 pages in question removed from current copies of the book. The ruling also prohibited the publisher from using any portions of the extracted material in future publications. Damages of 10,000 DM were awarded to Spitz and Höttl was forced to publicly retract his remarks, an ironic twist considering the eliminated assertions reportedly represented one of the few instances of accuracy between the book's covers. Despite the favourable ruling however, Spitz was unable to shake off the effects of the adverse publicity. Spurred by material that surfaced during the court proceedings, officials with the Bavarian Department of Justice decided to keep an eye on him. Once enough evidence had been gathered, a subpoena was delivered to Spitz's Munich villa on October 13th, 1956. In a stunning performance that outshone any of Höttl's elaborate exit strategies, Spitz's response to the impending prosecution was to die of a timely heart attack the very same day.

Another irked over the limelight *"Unternehmen Bernhard's"* release had created, was Bernhard Krüger himself. One of the entries Krüger took issue with was the claim he had simply returned home to Hannover after the war, living there quietly under his own name, while Interpol heatedly searched the world for his whereabouts. Höttl's scenario contrasted sharply with other versions of Krüger's post-war adventures, which alternately portrayed him as having escaped to Italy, working as a banker in Buenos Aires, or committing suicide in an English jail. Krüger's actual saga had been much more banal. Captured shortly after the German collapse, he was held by the Americans until escaping custody in November 1946. Re-captured a short time later, he was placed under the supervision of the OSS until 1949, at which time he once again managed to take flight. With the help of an old colleague, he managed to find sanctuary in Dassel, a town north-west of Göttingen, Germany. Able to obtain work at the Hahnemühle Paper factory, he disappeared for seven years. That seclusion was suspended on August 23rd 1956, when Krüger released a statement admitting his role as a technical advisor to OB, and refuting Höttl's claims about the criminality of OB prison workers. Hoping the declaration would clear both his name and conscience, Krüger was dismayed to learn the expired Statute of Limitations he presumed would protect him from prosecution, applied only to his direct involvement in OB, leaving him vulnerable to be charged with other alleged crimes. To his fortune, officials in the German Justice Department showed no interest in investigating his possible role in the murder of members of the counterfeiting unit who fell gravely ill, or the final liquidation order issued at Ebensee, prevented from being carried out by the timely arrival of American troops. Although no judicial proceedings were instigated, Krüger was convinced prosecutors were on his trail. Abandoning his Dassel refuge, he moved to the Stuttgart suburb of Krontal, slipping back into anonymity for another several years. His whereabouts was re-discovered by a State prosecutor in the early '60's, and a series of endeavours undertaken to bring him to justice. The numerous legal manoeuvres failed however, and on May 7th, 1965, all pending cases against him were dropped. No further attempts at prosecution were made, allowing Krüger to spend his remaining years in Hamburg, before dying there in 1984 at the age of 80.

As tempered as his own level of involvement appeared on the pages of 'Unternehmen Bernhard', Höttl had shown little restraint when it came to denoting the contributions of colleagues. Nowhere was that seepage more evident than with the activities of Friedrich *"Fritz"* Schwend. Like other former associates, Schwend did not appreciate being *"venerated"* in print, especially after having specifically warned his old friend on the risks of broadcasting his memories too openly. Schwend reportedly wrote to Höttl in the early '50's, relating how while in British custody, investigating officers had informed him that higher authorities were intent on denying the existence of OB and the damages it had caused. Anyone prepared to claim otherwise, he was warned, either in a book or a public statement, would in the words of British officials, *"be dealt with accordingly"*. Höttl chose to ignore Schwend's subtle advice, defiantly writing in his book that he too had been grilled by British prosecutors at Nuremberg, and as a consequence was left with the distinct impression the British considered counterfeiting a legitimate weapon of war, and wished to prosecute only those who were active in the distribution network, i.e. people like Schwend.

Given the sheer volume of text Höttl devoted to Schwend, technically still a fugitive at the time of the its release, it was inevitable speculation would arise over Höttl's level of collusion in Schwend's post-war intrigues. One set of clues to this involvement could be traced back to late 1944, when Schwend, alias Dr. Wendig, alias Bernter, alias Wenceslas Turi, alias Don Federico, alias Federico Schwend, had reportedly been preparing for his future with a series of large deposits to banks in Trieste and Switzerland. The deposits in question had allegedly been made with the aid of several trusted agents, one of whom was thought to have been Friedrich H. Carl Karnatz.

Born March 1, 1908, Karnatz had been stationed in the economic section of Amt VI, when Höttl arranged for him to be seconded to work with Schwend's network. During his time with Schwend, an appreciable amount of trust developed between the two men, so much so that in March 1945, Schwend reportedly entrusted Karnatz to travel to Switzerland to deposit 100,000 Turkish £'s, 200,000 Danish Krone, and a large sum of Belgian Francs into a secret Swiss account in his name. Schwend's trust appears to have been somewhat premature. Instead of returning to deliver the deposit receipt as arranged, Karnatz simply disappeared.

According to Höttl, Schwend had also been the victim of a second swindle, this one perpetrated by an agent named Theopil Kamber. Unlike Karnatz however, Kamber's plot to abscond to the Balkans with a supply of fake £ notes was uncovered, resulting in his murder. (Two decades later, Schwend would be accused of having participated in the planning of Kamber's death, and sentenced in absentia to 21 years imprisonment by an Italian court in Bolzano.)

Despite these two apparent setbacks, there was enough treasure leftover for Schwend to have allegedly buried 80 kilograms of gold, $80,000 US, and 100,000 Swiss Francs in a valley in southwestern Austria, before heading off to meet with Höttl in Alt Aussee. It was while the two were discussing their immediate futures, the decision was made to dispatch yet another courier to Switzerland. The envoy this time was an individual named Ferry Manser, a friend of Schwend's from their days together in Abbazia. Instructed to travel to Lugano, he was to deposit some 300,000 Swiss Francs in a Credit Union, informing bank officials there, the money was to be forwarded to an account in Geneva. As it happened Manser had not been able to complete his mission before Schwend fled to South America. As with many chronicled escapes, versions on the circumstances leading up to Schwend's hasty departure and Höttl's possible role in it, vary. One account had him captured by the Americans shortly after the end of hostilities. Transferred to Munich, he was believed to have used forged papers to identify himself as an officer in the German Army. Suspicious that *"Major Kemp"* was not who he claimed to be, the Americans were attempting to establish whether their prisoner was guilty of any punishable offences, when former OB operative, Georg Spitz showed up and began making discreet inquiries about his interned boss. Utilizing his own contacts within the American intelligence service, Spitz managed to have a message relayed to Schwend, the essence of which warned that if Schwend wasn't prepared to relinquish a substantial amount of his alleged treasure, he would never make it out of jail alive. According to sources, this purported scenario concluded with Schwend, Spitz, and two American officials, travelling to the Kaunertal valley in southwestern Austria, to retrieve a cache of buried gold, before going their separate ways.

A second version of events implied that Schwend had been enticed into working for the CIC while in custody in Munich. This theory claimed he convinced US officials of his loyalty just long enough to make good his escape in early 1946. Once underground, he managed to obtain a travel visa as well as several International Red Cross documents identifying him as a Croatian by the name Wenceslav Turi. While the visa had reportedly been supplied by a Vatican connection, the Red Cross documents had come from Jaac van Harten, a Dutch-born Jew active on behalf of the Red Cross in Budapest in 1944, and a financial advisor to SS Colonel and Nazi entrepreneur, Kurt Becher. Van Harten later became one of Schwend's top OB agents in Hungary, a career move reportedly instigated by his acquaintance, Wilhelm Höttl.

Höttl: 1945
"At that time I made the acquaintance of a Dutchman by the name of Jaac van Harten. He asked for my intervention on behalf of certain Jewish families in Budapest so as to avoid deportation into Germany. Partly I was successful to get for those people immigration visas into neutral states, Sweden, and so on, and Turkey. I worked together with Harten all of the time in Budapest, but as soon as the Jewish action had been extended into Budapest, and he being a Jew himself, was endangered by it, I brought him into Meran, which was the border between upper Tyrol and northern Italy."

Despite his various attempts to secure his future, Schwend appears to have departed Europe without much of his reputed assets. Once in Peru, he endeavoured to get a bead on the men who had disappeared with *"his"* money. He soon discovered one of them was living in neighbouring Chile under the name of Carlo Bentien. Since his arrival, Karnatz had been able to gain a strong foothold in the Chilean business community, rising to become a member of the board of directors of the German-South American bank, a daughter company of the Deutsche Bank. Suspecting that some of 'his' missing funds may have aided Karnatz's rise to prominence, Schwend contacted the German Embassy in Santiago in hopes of obtaining more information. Whatever pretext he offered proved plausible enough for Embassy officials to discuss the matter with Karnatz. Several weeks later, Schwend was informed Karnatz denied having siphoned off any of the disputed money, maintaining he did not return the deposit slip as he had believed the funds belonged to the Reich and not to one individual. Not long after issuing that statement, Karnatz managed to acquire a German passport from the Bonn government, and returned to Germany to take up work for the Deutsche-South America bank in Hamburg.

Details of Manser's post-Geneva exploits emerged after Schwend engaged the services a German lawyer in Buenos Aires to carry out an investigation. Contacting several individuals in Europe, amongst whom was Höttl, the lawyer eventually determined Manser had not betrayed his boss, but simply employed a technique used by many Nazi couriers in Switzerland, of depositing the money under a non-German name to avoid detection and possible investigation by Swiss authorities. In the end, the information turned out to be somewhat academic as any attempts to gain access to the account, either directly or through a middleman, would have involved considerable risk. As a result, the alleged cache, as well as numerous other Swiss accounts of questionable origin, reportedly remained untouched.

Höttl: 1945

"For years now I am suffering from an ulcerated stomach, caused by a nervous stomach complaint and am subject to regular periodical attacks in spring and late autumn."

In the decade since that complaint was uttered at Nuremberg, few changes in lifestyle had been instituted to alleviate that chronic ailment. If anything, the turbulence created by assorted court appearances, school responsibilities and familial duties had increased Höttl's vulnerability to random attacks. Such was the case in the spring of 1956, when word arrived that Hungarian authorities had once again submitted a formal request to the Austrian Government for his extradition. Branding him a leading figure in the Nazi intelligence service, the Hungarians not only accused Höttl of having participated in the mass arrests of Hungarian patriots in March 1944, but also with the preparations and implementation of the Fascist putsch that October, crimes which under Hungarian law were punishable by death or a long prison term. Some pundits believed the Hungarian move had been spurred by the publicity surrounding the release of Unternehmen Bernhard. Others believed it had more to do with hopes of finding an Austrian government more amenable to seeing Höttl brought to justice. Those hopes were pinned to the changes brought about by Austria's independence in 1955, a feature of which was reduced American influence in Austrian affairs. Hungarian officials had laid the blame for the rejection of their 1946 extradition bid on American interference. Although that obstacle had been substantially reduced with Austrian independence, what the Hungarians failed to take into account was that in the interim, former Nazis had been allowed to officially re-claim their citizenship as part of the country's new status. Matters weren't helped when official discussions regarding the extradition case took place behind closed doors, causing many observers in and out of Austria, to believe the government had something to hide. One rumour to have swept through political corridors in Vienna arose from Höttl's well known practise of keeping files, some of which had reportedly come to light in the search of his premises during the Ponger/Verber affair. Reported to date back to pre-Anschluss days, the discovered documents were alleged to have contained information that could prove highly embarrassing to individuals now active in government and business circles. Whether there was any real substance to the rumours or not, the mere thought of an embittered Höttl revealing material from the confines of a Hungarian jail cell, worked greatly to his advantage.

Once the diplomatic and legal wrangling between the two governments had ceased, notice of the decision to deny the request was relayed to Hungarian officials. Couched in diplomatic jargon, the reasoning for the rejection was that Höttl had merely been accused of 'supporting' the installation of the Szalasi government and not with any 'blood crimes'. As relieved as Höttl was by the ruling, the threat of extradition was not the only trouble to test his faulty metabolism that summer.

Völker Höttl: 2000
"I recall it so clearly because in 1956 we were living in thisbig house in Alt Aussee. Each night there were noises outside around the house, and my mother insisted that he, my father, no longer walk home from work, that he be picked up. I was 14 at the time and on one side found it suspenseful, and on the other hand I was afraid. From time to time packages arrived, which we immediately passed on to the State Security officials, because nobody could be sure whether or not there were explosives inside. They made efforts. In one of the books at his house there was a report about someone having watched the house. It was a Hungarian. They wanted to get their hands on him."

Völker Höttl's comments were backed up by the observations of long time Bad Aussee resident, Josef Grafl. The last surviving member of the Resistance quartet parachuted into Ausseerland in the spring of 1945, Grafl claimed Höttl had at times appeared anxious his past would one day catch up with him, especially, as Grafl put it, through old colleagues who knew enough about his exploits to incriminate him.

If Höttl had been unnerved by the shadow of Hungarian justice, he did his best not to let it show or hamper his ability to carry out his duties as school director. Although the negative attention generated by the extradition hearing did not have any discernible impact on the school, details of the case had been duly noted by critics in the Education Ministry, and set aside for battles still to come.

Much as Höttl had predicted, the bestowal of the Öffentliche Recht in June 1956 opened the doors to a dramatic increase in the school's enrolment. By the beginning of the 1960 school year, the Bad Aussee emporium had grown to encompass almost 400 students, 300 of which were non-residents. Drawn from all over Austria and Germany, students and staff were housed in seven separate buildings. To meet the enduring demand for accommodation, Höttl and his associates continued to purchase or lease additional space, eventually amassing a total of nine buildings, including the villa Schloss Ramsgut in Bad Aussee and three structures in Alt Aussee. According to Höttl, much of the school's continuing success could be placed at the feet of its 'new' director, Dr. Hans Mühlbacher.

An experienced teacher and administrator, Mühlbacher's three year term had commenced in early 1956, following Elfriede Höttl's decision to relinquish the position she had held since the school's inception. Reportedly admired and respected by staff and students alike, Mühlbacher oversaw the overall expansion in the school's fortunes, climaxing with the completion of a new facility adjacent to the Villa Margit, just in time for the fall term of 1960. Staff for all the facilities, which included teachers, service personnel and hand workers, had surged to forty people, making the school one of the largest employers in the region, second only to the Salt Mines. With the exception of various religious schools, Höttl's enterprise was thought to be the largest private school in the country. But despite the growing enrolment and monthly student fees as high as 1,500 Austrian Schillings, Höttl was often heard to complain about having to abide by a tight operating budget. Mühlbacher had been encouraged to look for ways of reducing costs and one of his ideas was the creation of an agricultural co-op, located on a local farm site. Originally owned by the Meier family, all of whom later perished in a concentration camp, the "Bartelshof" was Aryanized in 1936. At the time Höttl and his family took up residence in 1957, the farmhouse was reportedly owned by a Herr Christ. Although Höttl would be forced to vacate the house in 1959, when an inheritance investigation ordered the property returned to a relative of the Meier family, in the intervening two years, the farming co-op had proven to be a large success, housing over thirty cows, fifty pigs and between two and three hundred chickens at it's peak. All of farm's profits were used to help defray expenses on provisions needed for the school's Internat.

Along with the school's increasing influence within the community however, came a good deal of controversy. Already dogged by rumours of dubious practises being behind its eclipsing success, questions started to arise over the quality and origin of the school's teaching staff and curriculum.

In the period immediately following the conclusion of the war, one of the difficult problems faced by the provisional government in Austria was the introduction of a credible de-Nazification program. The logistical nightmare of investigating the wartime activities of each of 540,000 officially registered members of the NSDAP was virtually an impossible task. Even attempts at launching a re-education program on a more minor scale were met with resistance by a society reticent to prosecute the *"Mitläufer"* in its midst. Although numerous Party members were incarcerated, others scrutinized by the de-Nazification program often tended to face less punitive actions. One example was teachers and university professors, who if confirmed as having been active Party members, were ostracized, suspended or banned outright from resuming teaching posts held before the war.

Andrea Hofer: 2002
"Father had a good friend, Professor Borodajkewycz. He was a fanatical anti-semite, also long after the war. Although he was someone who never denied the Holocaust, he claimed that it hadn't been so many. Father had countered with a remark that 'it didn't matter whether it was 6 million or 1.6 million or whatever, each was one too many'. From this point on all contact was broken off."

An apparent exception ot the rule, Borodajkewycz had been allowed to return to teaching at the International Trade Academy in Vienna in 1954, albeit under the watchful eye of the Education Ministry, then headed by Heinrich Drimmel. More incorrigible than many educational authorities had presumed, he used that forum to deliver a number of anti-semitic, neo-Nazi and anti-democratic speeches. Despite these sporadic exhibitions of his ideology, no action was taken to remove him. It wasn't until the onset of bloody student demonstrations against Borodajkewycz in 1960 that Education Minister Theodor Piffl-Percevic moved to temporarily suspend him. Re-instated not long after, Borodajkewycz continued to spread his reactionary leanings for another five years, until the death of a protester at another demonstration in 1966, finally forced him into retirement. The removal of his academic pulpit however, did not stop him from spouting his rhetoric, and he continued to write articles for the right wing press right up until his death in 1984.

A second educator reportedly barred from the classroom was Dr. Hans Roithner, the Private Mittelschule's deputy-director. Roithner's membership in the NSDAP had precipitated his suspension from teaching until 1947. While it may not have been an overt policy on Höttl's part to recruit from such a pool of disenfranchised teachers, a Nazi past was apparently no deterrent to employment at his school. Beyond the advantages of working with like-minded colleagues, hiring such individuals presented the prospect of employees being more compliant or beholden, given that opportunities elsewhere were limited. It was also not lost on Höttl, how such a gesture of 'tolerance' on his part, could strengthen his status within the subterranean Nazi community. Evidence that at least a portion of Höttl's teaching staff still held Nazi beliefs emerged from several sources. Former friend and colleague, Fritz Fischer, interviewed in 1999, bluntly stated it was simply a given that a number of old Nazi functionaries worked at the school. Höttl's daughter, Andrea was more specific, citing the example of Professor Friedrich Rötzer, a Bad Aussee native, she described as having been *"an outstanding instructor in Latin and German,"* but also definitely someone with a Nazi past. Other former students came forward to relate how certain instructors had often used the classroom as a subtle podium for their *"former"* beliefs. Whether or not the school was as much a haven for former Nazis as some critics depicted, questions about staff orientation and curriculum direction did not appear to affect enrolment. What was apparently of more interest for many wealthy, conservative parents was the school's reputed propensity for graduating students who had been unable to obtain their diplomas elsewhere. It was the induction of such students that eventually saddled the school with the label, *'Fliegeschule'*, an expression loosely interpreted as a venue where expelled or failing students stood a better chance of achieving their Matura, and would not be held back merely because of academic shortcomings.

Over the years, other attributes would come to attach themselves to the school's reputation, few more solidly anchored than the allegation that a discreet donation to the school's administrative fund could result in a coinciding improvement in a respective student's scholastic standing. For the most part, it was an aspersion Höttl chose to ignore. Despite the occasional avowal that a Matura from his institution could only be obtained through hard work and study, the nagging perception endured, strengthened by an article in the May 7th, issue of the Austrian magazine, PROFIL in 1984. The story recounted how a student in the 1950's, had landed in Höttl's Internat after having been expelled from a series of other schools. The student in question claimed the move had come as a result of stories his mother had heard of how effective a well-placed endowment could be. He went on to back that assertion by providing the magazine with material that illustrated how he had been promoted from the 5th class to the 6th, without having produced passing grades. Höttl's response to the article came in an open letter to the editor of a local paper, in which he claimed his own reputation and that of the school's had been besmirched by 'Profil's' erroneous reports. Rather than ending the matter, Höttl's remarks prompted another former student to step forward. No sooner had Franz Amon confirmed the first student's accusations, Höttl decided to sue. In the ensuing squabble, lawyers for both two former students produced several witnesses, each of whom was prepared to corroborate their clients' stories. In addition to the collected affidavits, lawyers also saw fit to prepare a detailed outline of Höttl's backg-round prior to his involvement with the school. Although the document was not released to the public, a copy was leaked to Höttl. Shortly thereafter, face-saving negotiations were initiated with the opposing lawyers. When attempts at a settlement failed, Höttl simply withdrew the lawsuit, citing health factors as the reason for doing so.

In May 2006, the same student who had supplied information for the original PROFIL article, took advantage of a television interview with ARTE, (German-French television network) to add another critique of his time spent at Höttl's school. Now a well known Austrian entertainer of Je-wish heritage, Andre Heller recalled the trauma of his first day when Höttl introduced him to the class with a warning not to sit near the new student, as he *"had evil blood flowing through his veins"*.

By the end of the 1950's, most residents of Ausseerland had come to feel the economic boost the school provided to the community. Most had believed those benefits, as well as the opportunities it presented for their own children's education, far outweighed any negative ballast it may have accumulated. Education Ministry officials in Vienna however, had viewed things differently. Having kept a cautious watch on Höttl's enterprise for some time, in late 1959, they concluded a closer inspection of the facilities was fully warranted. Coming forward to speak in the school's defence, various townspeople cited the high number of prominent graduates who had populated its classrooms since its inception. That legacy was especially true in the field of sport, with the short distance runner, Gerd Noster, the champion water skier, Bernd Rauchenwald, as well as Formula One World race car champions, Jochen Rindt, and Niki Lauda amongst the alumni. In addition to those figures, many leading doctors, economists, university professors and high ranking civil servants, were trotted out in support of the school. One alumnus in particular, Prof. Dr. Dr. Peter Schachner-Blazizek, was a rising political star who would go on to become the Deputy Premier for the Austrian State of Steiermark, and later play an integral role in seeing that his former school master receive the official recognition he felt he deserved.

In spite of the host of notables on parade, the tide of negative impressions continued. As a result, in the spring of 1960, the State School Board, presumably with the Ministry's approval, moved to install Dr. Gunther Legat as the school's new director. Although his mandate was primarily to oversee the running of the institution, Legat was also expected to investigate certain 'irregularities' within its administrative practises. Despite persistent bickering, disagreements and intrigues between Legat and Höttl, conditions at the school over the next few months were said to have noticeably improved. In the midst of those battles, in February 1961, Höttl tried to flex the authority he presumed to still possess, by announcing his intention to replace Legat with retired Steiermark State advisor, Dr. Bruno Stettinger. Questioned by a local journalist as to whether the school board would be satisfied with Stettinger's appointment, Höttl's response was, "No, but that doesn't matter." (Volksstimme, 10.5.1961) Thirty five years later, the extent of the simmering hostility between Legat and Höttl was still evident. Writing in his final post-war memoir in 1996, Höttl bitterly claimed Legat had done little more than spy on him during his tenure, generally undermining the school's reputation, and reporting his findings back to officials in Vienna. Legat's dismissal on March 16th did little to resolve the fundamental problems facing the school. If anything matters worsened and within six months Stettinger had vacated his stool to be replaced by the Ministry's appointee, Dr. Carl Schediwy. According to Höttl, Schediwy's term, which lasted until the end of the 1961/62 school year, did nothing more than sustain a complete aura of instability, causing further damage to the school's credibility. Fed up with the chaos created by the revolving directorships and the less than comprehensive curriculum being offered, Federal and State Education Boards decided to revoke the right for the school's teachers to conduct final exams. By assuring that individual teachers no longer had sole control to evaluate the merits of a student's efforts, officials hoped to eliminate the threat of *"manipulated grades"*. Students eligible to write their Matura could still take their exams at the school, but were now required to do so before a Commission selected by Board officials. By that point however, imposing changes had already become somewhat academic. Continuing problems at the school, as well as Höttl's overweening belief in his ability to outflank Ministry officials, had kept him from recognizing how a seemingly unrelated event in Argentina one year earlier, had managed to jar the fate of the school on to an irreversible course.

Shortly after stepping off a bus near his home in a Buenos Aires suburb on the evening of May 11th, 1960, Adolf Eichmann was seized by Israeli agents and hustled off to a secret location. Twelve days later, Israeli officials announced the notorious fugitive's capture, informing the public he was now in a Israeli jail cell awaiting trial for his role in the Holocaust. Reverberations from the announcement were felt around the world, yet Höttl appeared to take the news in stride, convinced the event was not likely to create any difficulties for himself. Adopting a policy of watch and wait whenever questioned by local journalists, he maintained the last he had seen or heard from Eichmann was on the streets of Alt Aussee in 1945. Israeli officials however, had been more interested in Höttl than he assumed. Citing portions of Höttl's testimony given at Nuremberg on November 5th and 26th, 1945, Gideon Hausner, the Attorney General of Israel, advised his colleagues, the person behind the statements was still alive and available for questioning. Despite his awareness of Hungary's failed attempts to extradite Höttl, records indicate Hausner initially considered trying to force Höttl to testify in Jerusalem. Aside from the expected Austrian resistance to any extradition request, Hausner's position was further complicated by the fact Höttl knew his membership in the SS made him liable for prosecution under Israeli law. In an attempt to counter that 'obstacle', Hausner managed to convince Israeli prosecutors to offer immunity should Höttl agree to attend the trial. Israeli prosecutors however, were not the only ones interested in having Höttl present in Jerusalem. Known for having defended several prominent Nazis at Nuremberg, Eichmann's counsel, Dr. Robert Servatius was interested in exploring Höttl's potential usefulness to the defence. In spite of the apparent clamour for his testimony, Höttl was not prepared to testify for, against, or as he had put it in Nuremberg, even 'about' his former colleague. Mindful of the fact Eichmann had technically been kidnapped by Israel's Intelligence Service,(-Mossad), he had no intention of putting himself at risk on the basis of Israeli promises. Alluding to his ill health, he formally declined invitations from both parties to attend the trial. Facing what threatened to be a long-drawn out battle to evaluate the true state of Höttl's health, Israeli prosecutors changed tack, agreeing to have him testify by affidavit from Bad Aussee. Forty years later, in a moment of candour, Höttl's daughter disclosed that as a 15 year old, she had been confused by her father's decision to forego what she felt was an opportunity to set the record straight.

Andrea Hofer(Höttl): 2002

"Why,… if it was proven that he had helped a number of Jews, would he have anything to fear by going there? They would have seen him as one who had tried to help. So why would he be in danger there? I never understood that."

Höttl had rarely, if ever, spoken openly with his children about aspects of his wartime activities, suggesting the story of his alleged Samaritanism had come from another source.

Andrea Hofer(Höttl): 2002

"This was one of the few times she spoke of it,… because in general she never discussed these matters… ever. I can tell you that one time my mother, through some adventurous methods, had visited my father in Nuremberg to give him something. She said that someone had more or less helped to smuggle her across the border into Germany and that it had been a Jewish family. My mother said she had wanted to give them a ring or something for assisting her, but the family had refused, saying ' no, your husband helped us at one time, so we won't accept anything'. This episode reportedly took place in 1946 or 1947…… It was something out of the ordinary because she never spoke of such things."

In an attempt to allay her confusion, Andrea had belatedly approached her father for an explanation. Answering in what she described as a gruff manner, he told her the subject was simply not open for discussion. Höttl's refusal to clarify matters seems all the more puzzling in light of the fact he had previously used other forums to infer precisely what she was seeking to confirm.

Höttl: 1946

"During this time (in Budapest) I tried to help Eichmann where I could and he tried to help me. He helped me free numerous Jews…one day in the summer of 1944, the well known Austrian film star Marta Harell came to me and asked me for help. It had to do with the wife of the actor Hans Moser, a

Jewess who was a well known personality living in Budapest. When the Hungarians introduced these race laws, she was sent to a transfer depot to be sent to the East. I contacted Eichmann in Budapest and told him about this case. I made up a story about the Führer often watching Moser films at night. He immediately obtained Frau Moser's freedom from the Hungarians and had her taken to Switzerland. That was a typical approach by Eichmann. The Führer watched Moser films,…therefore nothing should happen to Frau Moser. In Nuremberg I became friends with Hitler's adjutant (Julius) Schaub and he told me that Hitler really had watched Moser films. So it turned out that what I had merely invented was true and through that Frau Moser was rescued… It was his art, to serve those above him, to make himself liked by his superiors. And that explains a lot. Eichmann wasn't a thief or a murderer. That's not correct. I knew him too well."

Prior to 1960, using Eichmann to describe one's own *'courageous acts'* had represented little risk. Following his capture however, Eichmann was in a position to expound on Höttl's knowledge 'about the business', thereby threatening to inadvertently satisfy Andrea's curiosity once and for all.

In the eleven months between his arrest and the start of the trial, Eichmann had been interrogated at length by Capt. Avner Werner Less of the Israeli Police. More than capable of recalling most of his Nazi career in great detail, the former 'organizing specialist's' memory seemed to falter when asked to elaborate on the nature of his association with Höttl.

Eichmann: 1961

"I met Höttl in Berlin. I don't remember the circumstances. I believe he too, was in the SD... I can't say at the present moment whether Höttl was in Hungary. If he was, I must have spoken with him there... I think Höttl had long been a department head in Section VI of the Reich Security Headquarters. He knew about as much about the business as I did. Section VI was an intelligence outfit. So naturally they knew all about the activities of their ...... well, of their own organization".

After months of preparation and manoeuvring, Eichmann's trial began on April 11th, 1961 in Jerusalem. Facing a total of 15 charges, including crimes against humanity, Eichmann viewed the entire courtroom proceedings from inside a bulletproof glass booth specially built for him. Approximately two months later, official papers from the District Court of Jerusalem arrived in Bad Aussee, commanding Höttl to appear at a hearing scheduled for June 19th. Initially designated to be open to the public, the proceedings were abruptly moved behind closed doors following a hastily called meeting between parties on the first morning. Identifying himself as a 46 year old married Roman Catholic, and administrator of the Bad Aussee Private secondary school, Höttl was placed under oath before the charges against Eichmann were read out to the court. Over the next three days, seventy-five questions were put to Höttl, forty-five of which were from the defence. Not in a position to know what information Eichmann may have divulged to his captors prior to the start of the trial, Höttl chose to implement a strategy of limited restraint, repeatedly begging the court's patience for his inability to recall details. He began by telling the court his first encounter with the defendant had occurred in March 1938, not long after Eichmann had arrived in Vienna to organize the emigration of Austrian Jews. Despite the fact that Eichmann had testified otherwise, local court officials overlooked the discrepancy, urging Höttl to focus on Eichmann's personality. Portraying him as a conscientious and efficient organizer who had *"streamlined"* the entire emigration process under one roof, Höttl testified that any dealings he had with Eichmann at the time had been in connection with the his role as head of the Central Office for Emigration.

As the proceedings rolled on, observers couldn't help but notice that much of what Höttl dredged up from the past, fell into the legal limbo of *"Aussage gegen Aussage"* in relation to Eichmann's own declarations. That was particularly evident when it came to explanations on who bore responsibility for organizing the deportation of the Jews in Hungary. Höttl's version claimed Eichmann and his special commando group had operated independently from other German authorities, ie. the SS and SD, in carrying out the evacuations. Eichmann however, had previously told Israeli interrogators it had been the evacuating authority that had drawn up the lists of people destined for 'special treatment', lists that presumably were compiled with the assistance of the SS and SD. While these two statements and many others that followed were not completely contradictory, such *"Unklarheit"* makes it difficult to gage what impact Höttl's testimony had on the outcome of the trial. The same could not be said in reverse.

Although little if any of Eichmann's testimony concerning Höttl could be considered legally incriminating, the intense media attention that engulfed the case, once again made him a widespread topic of conversation. Lured by the media spotlight created by persistent reporters eager to learn more about his relationship with Eichmann, Höttl's pride eventually got the better of him, leading him to make several errors in judgment, the most serious of which was agreeing to be interviewed for an American magazine. Published under the title, *"My Friend Eichmann"*, the subsequent article exposed a number of intimate details about their friendship, including how Eichmann had suffered from an inferiority complex, compounded by his hatred of the fact that he looked Jewish. Needless to say, publicly acknowledging his proximity to Eichmann did little to improve the school's beleaguered reputation. Officials at the Ministry of Education, already perturbed by Legat's dismissal as well as their findings from previous inspections, found the notoriety around the Eichmann trial and Höttl's latest bout of candour too much to bear. They decided to launch a formal investigation of all aspects of the school and its director with particular interest given to the institution's current financial status. Despite the significant resources at its disposal, which over the years had reportedly included book royalties, monies saved during Höttl's stint with the CIC and more recently consultant fees purportedly paid to him by several film companies interested in making films about the Nazis, the school had somehow amassed a deficit to the tune of one million Austrian Schilling. That, investigators would soon discover, was the not the only problem facing the school. As they continued to delve deeper into its affairs, the longer the trail of improprieties to emerge. Teachers practicing without the required certification, 'voluntary healthy farm work' being performed by students on Höttl's properties, 'night vacation permits' obtainable for the higher classes, diploma swindles and unsubstantiated firings, represented the proverbial tip of the iceberg. Höttl denied knowledge of the alleged wrong doings, but the truth was little went on at the school that wasn't partial to his control or approval. In spite of his efforts to contain the investigation, reports about the school's *"customary procedures"* eventually leaked out to local and national publications. In one particular article, reference was made to a *'superior'* having forced a teacher to rescind the failing grade given to the son of a prominent civil servant, and replace it with a more satisfactory mark. Although the *'superior'* in question went unnamed, the implication was clear where the order had originated. A second report centred on accusations two of the school's teachers had revealed the contents of upcoming exams to a number of their students, presumably for some form of compensation.

Despite what seemed to be an unorthodox method of *"financing"* their children's education, the system in place at Höttl's school was not unique. Similar practices had reportedly existed at a number of other expensive private schools in Austria. What made the Bad Aussee institution stand out was the fact that despite the considerable sums invested by parents, scholastic results often fell far short of expectations. According to statistics uncovered by Ministry investigators, of fifty-six students recently eligible to write their Matura, only nineteen actually managed to graduate.

Burdened by the combination of a heavy debt load and allegations of mismanagement, prospects for a quick turnaround continued to look bleak. To make matters worse, on July 11th.1961, an issue of the Neue Österreich newspaper announced the school had been unable to meet its payroll since May. Fourteen of the teaching staff had been informed they were not scheduled to return for the fall semester. Now teetering on the brink of bankruptcy, Höttl attempted to extricate himself from his financial morass by soliciting a one time donation of five thousand Schillings from each parent. Not surprisingly, the idea was met with little enthusiasm and quickly abandoned.

As innuendo and rebuttal continued to ricochet between Höttl and the press throughout the summer of 1961, events which may have otherwise gone unnoticed were now subjected to intense scrutiny. An example of that increased interest surfaced in the June 8th edition of the *"Volksstimme"* newspaper, which reported on Höttl's involvement with a man by the name of Schwarzbauer. Described as resident of Barcelona, Schwarzbauer was alleged to have arrived in Ausseerland in the spring of 1961 with a plan to recover the *'legendary'* treasure from the Toplitzsee. Aware of Albrecht Gaiswinkler's previous attempt to retrieve the trove, Schwarzbauer had initially approached the former resistance fighter with a proposal to work collectively. According to Gaiswinkler, cited as the source of the story, Schwarzbauer told him he would be free to keep all gold, jewels or money discovered, provided he (Schwarzbauer) alone would retain the secret RSHA lists reputedly sunk with the treasure. Suspicious that Schwarzbauer was merely a front man, Gaiswinkler used his own contacts to try and learn who else might be behind the renewed interest in the documents. Not only did Gaiswinkler learn Schwarzbauer was a former SS officer believed to be in the employ of a Western Intelligence Service, but also that while in Ausseerland, he was residing as a guest at Höttl's school. Although the project was abandoned following Gaiswinkler's rejection of the offer, the episode raised questions about the identities of other *"guests"* frequenting the villa. What was of much more concern to Höttl however, were articles spawned by continuing leaks from the Eichmann interrogations. Initially, he had not paid much notice to stories related to his activities in Hungary, but that complacency was shaken when a national newspaper reported that Hungarian officials were again preparing documents to extradite him. As in their previous two attempts, the grounds for this extradition order were Höttl's alleged involvement in the preparation of lists used in the arrest of hundreds of Hungarian patriots, and his participation in the installation of the Szalasi government. Several weeks later, Justice Ministry officials in Vienna informed Höttl the reports of Hungary's intentions were accurate. Still reluctant to interpret the news as a serious threat, Höttl wrote to Ministry officials repeating his claims of innocence, admonishing them for what he felt was the *"slander campaign"* against him, and the potential damage to his current negotiations with school officials. He attempted to buttress his position by pointing out that despite a detailed examination of his Hungarian activities at Nuremberg, no charges had ever been laid. Hoping to further deflate rumours of an impending extradition order, he wrote to the editor that published the original story.

Höttl: Feb. 25th, 1961

"During this time (1944) I did everything in my power as a German officer and Austrian patriot to prevent the Hungarian Army from surrendering to the Russians. The success of Horthy's plan (to seek a separate peace with the Soviets) would have meant the complete overrunning of Hungary by the Red Army in the fall of 1944 and an advance as far as Vienna by Christmas of that year. As an Austrian, I am proud to acknowledge that through my reporting as an officer of the Secret Service, this plan was thwarted."

Höttl's statement was in effect an admission of what he had previously denied, a fact that did not go unnoticed by Hungarian authorities. In what was likely an attempt to stir up public indignation, reports of Höttl's alleged criminal activity began to surface in the government controlled press. One of the most damning articles appeared in the *"Magyar Nemzet"* on 28.3.61, fingering Höttl as one of sixteen German officers who had been designated to receive the Holy Hungarian Crown medal for their assistance in Szalasi's takeover. Reacting in the Austrian media, Höttl attempted to shift emphasis away from whether he had merited such an award, by swearing he never received it, a claim technically correct given that he had been back in Austria when the medals were presented on Dec. 18th, 1944.

Höttl: 1961

"I declare once again that in no way was I involved in the power struggle action of the Arrow Cross people, which was best proven by the new Hungarian Foreign Minister, Baron Dr. Kemeny. Kemeny wrote to Kaltenbrunner shortly after the new government took office, explaining I was no longer welcome in Hungary. As far as an award having been given to me by the Hungarian government as thank you for my support of the Putsch, not one word is true."

In his haste to use Kemeny's remarks as clarification however, Höttl chose to ignore or had forgotten his own testimony at Nuremberg, in which he admitted to having arranged Kemeny's evacuation from Budapest to Meran in early 1945, hardly the type of action undertaken on behalf of someone who had reportedly declared you a persona non grata several months earlier.

◆

As history had shown, building an airtight case against Höttl was an uphill battle, the chances for success having been further reduced by the fact that extradition of Nazi war criminals in general, was slowly being phased out as Cold War politics came to outweigh concerns for seeing justice served. Logic suggests the Hungarians would have been aware of that development and would not have gone to the trouble and expense, if they hadn't felt there was a realistic basis for achieving their goal. Some observers though, suspected the decision to launch the formal request had been motivated as much by a desire to expose and humiliate Höttl, as by any thoughts of actually bringing him to trial. Whatever their actual rationale, in the fall of 1961, the Municipal Court of Budapest issued a warrant for Höttl's arrest, officially charging him with having assisted in the mass arrest of Hungarian resistance fighters in 1944. In a sign Austrian officials might be willing to depart from their previous policy, the government in Vienna promised to conduct an thorough investigation before issuing a decision. For someone as familiar with *"the rules of the game"*as Höttl, news that an exception might be made to the practice of not extraditing their citizens to Communist regimes, should have been a disturbing development. As the Austrian government's investigation dragged on, it was apparent to all concerned, matters would not be brought to a swift conclusion. In the meantime, the media in both countries continued to offer detailed coverage of the case, taking special delight in highlighting rampant speculation that Vienna's stalling was due in part to Höttl's abiding status as a feared political liability.

Accustomed to the pace of international diplomacy, by April 1962, Hungarian patience was nonetheless wearing thin. On April 19th, an article in the Neue Österreich announced the Communist government in Budapest had issued a memorandum repeating their demand for Höttl's immediate extradition, backing their argument with the claim that new documents in their possession proved he had committed war crimes. In another article in the same issue, a speaker for the Hungarian Partisan Association was quoted as saying *"Höttl, has the blood of thousands of Hungarians on his hands, and must be brought to justice"*, adding that most of the new evidence had come from Höttl's German and Hungarian colleagues.

SS Gen. Edmund Veesenmayer: 1946
"In March 1944 when the German authorities arrested Hungarian politicians, Höttl had prepared lists available. He prepared them personally as far as I know."

Similar allegations had been made in 1946 by other former associates, all of whom had testified at the trial of Laszlo Baky. During the proceedings, SS Lt. General Otto Winklemann, former Hungarian Interior Minister Gabor Vanja and Hungarian General Eugen Oskar Ruskay all confirmed Höttl's close ties to the right wing party of Fidel Palffy, had provided him with access to Party files containing the names of anti-German activists. The trio alleged Höttl had combined those names with ones taken from his own files to prepare a comprehensive list of political opponents, then turned over to Kaltenbrunner. As a result of Höttl's actions, over 3000 Hungarian politicians, writers, journalists, officers and artists had been imprisoned, dozens of whom were tortured or murdered. A spokesman for the Partisan Association, said a second wave of arrests had taken place on October 19th, 1944. Described as even more deplorable than the first wave of arrests, that roundup had also been precipitated by a list purportedly prepared by Höttl. Claiming Austrian officials were aware of these incriminating documents, the article concluded by chastising their apparent unwillingness to act upon them.

Despite what many perceived as a growing momentum against Höttl, Austrian federal authorities ultimately decided to refuse the request. In explaining their judgement, they acknowledged Höttl's probable complicity, but said it could not be proven he had known the people arrested would be killed. As a result he could therefore only be accused of intelligence gathering, a treasonous offence from Hungary's perspective, but only punishable in Austria if proven to have been against Austrian interests. Having failed to bring Höttl to justice for the third consecutive time, the Hungarian government nonetheless chose to proceed with a trial. Found guilty of the charges against him, Höttl was subsequently sentenced to death in absentia.

Once the initial shock of being a condemned man had subsided, Höttl took the view that the government's decision had placed the bulk of his legal worries behind him. That sense of closure was interrupted a few days later however, with the arrival of yet another summons, this one requesting his testimony in a case against SS Lt. Col. Hermann Krumey and several other former Eichmann henchmen. Requested to testify in person in Frankfurt, Höttl revived the *"mitigating health circumstances"* that had exempted him from Jerusalem, to win permission to again testify from a Bad Aussee courtroom. Despite the fact that he and the main defendant were far from strangers, once proceedings got underway, Höttl professed to having only limited knowledge of Krumey's wartime activities.

Ten years Höttl's senior, Hermann Krumey was born in 1905 in the Moravian town of Schönberg, now part of the Czech Republic. A late recruit to the Nazi cavalcade, Krumey joined the SS in 1938, following the German union with Austria. From there he went on to serve as a Lieutenant Colonel in the Waffen SS, spending six months in the newly occupied Warthegau section of Poland, before moving on to the city of Lódz in mid 1940. As an appointee to the Security Police, he took part in operations to deport Jews from the city's ghetto to extermination camps in eastern Poland. In the summer of 1941 he was transferred to Croatia, where he participated in the rounding up of Jews into various internment camps. Here too, he was active in the deportation program, reportedly active in at least six separate train transports from Croatia to Auschwitz. As part of Eichmann's special commando group, he arrived in Hungary on March 19th, 1944, and was immediately assigned to help organize the Jewish Council, (Zsido Tanacs) in Budapest, setting the stage for the destruction that was to come in the ensuing months. As part of an agreement reached between Eichmann and the Council in June 1944, Krumey oversaw the transfer of some 21,000 Jews from Budapest to the Austrian internment camp at Strasshof.

Höttl: 1962

"The functionaries that I knew, the ones who were active in Budapest, to the best of my knowledge did not volunteer, but rather were sent there by their head offices. This was according to the internal departmental rules which stated that after a certain period, one had to either serve on the front or in a task

force, although that didn't necessarily mean that it had to be a special task force behind the front."

Most members of Eichmann's Hungarian commando however, were experienced *"specialists"* whose service in other occupied countries had helped *'refine'* the methods they were expected to apply to Hungarian Jewry. While none had volunteered for the assignment, an equal number had tried to evade it.

Accustomed to more rehearsed performances, observers at the trial were caught off guard by Höttl's openness. Many suspected it was rooted in his disgruntlement over the adverse publicity which had emanated from the Eichmann trial. Others believed his tongue had been loosened by the desire to settle the score with certain colleagues. Even though he himself had evaded justice numerous times, Höttl was resentful of the fact that many of the men who had issued negative statements about him during earlier trials in Hungary, had managed to return to respectable positions within German or Austrian business and society.

Höttl began his testimony on April 25th, 1962, initially following the same script used ten months prior. Acknowledging himself as a 47 year old married Catholic and father of three, residing at Puchen 36 in Alt Aussee, he led the court through an accounting of his time in Budapest, explaining how as the representative for Amt VI, his main duties had been to develop and maintain contact with Hungarian Intelligence Service to facilitate mutual espionage operations against the Russians. Turning to the period just before the German occupation, he told the court that critical information regarding Admiral Horthy's secret peace negotiations with the Soviets had come from the Hungarian leader's chief bodyguard, Peter Hain, implying therein that Hain had been the source of the infamous list. As further *'proof'* of Hain's complicity, Höttl revealed that for his services to the Reich, Hain had later been rewarded with appointment as head of the Hungarian Secret Service. What Höttl failed to mention at this juncture was that one month after his own arrival in Hungary, Himmler had promoted him (Höttl) to Major, presumably for his preliminary intelligence work in identifying anti-German collaborators.

Höttl then turned his sights of Dr. Edmund Vessenmayer, beginning with a description of the circumstances behind Veesenmayer's appointment as German envoy to Hungary in March 1944. According to Höttl, the

German Foreign Office, weakened by Hitler's acceptance of Höttl's plan to use German rather than Romanian troops to resolve the Hungarian problem, had attempted to strengthen its presence in the country by arranging for Veesenmayer's posting. Once in Budapest, Veesenmayer had endeavoured to exert his independence from the various SS offices, while at the same time trying to expand Foreign Office influence in matters that usually fell under the jurisdiction of the SS. One such area was *"the Jewish question,"* an issue for which, Veesenmayer had reportedly recommended the introduction of a Jewish Advisor.

Höttl: 1962

"As far as I'm concerned, considering that the Security Police and Eichmann's special commando were already deeply involved with the issue, the position of Jewish Advisor was fully superfluous. This tendency (of Veesenmayer) continued from day one of the German invasion. I can allow myself this accusation because I was also there from day one and previously had learned certain aspects about the preparations for the German action."

Although having reasserted Eichmann a leading role in the organizing and implementing of the deportation program, Höttl claimed he was still not the ultimate authority. Critical discussions with assorted Hungarian authorities on the issue were part of Eichmann's mandate, but the decisive talks with the Government and Horthy himself, had been led by Edmund Veesenmayer. Having ushered the Hungarians into the debate, Höttl reminded the court of the tacit collusion that had existed between the two 'partners'.

Höttl: 1962

"Before March 19th, 1944 certain persecution measures against the Jews had been implemented by the Hungarians. Prominent Jews left or were forced to leave the city, ostensibly to join labour forces. It was as a result of this measure that the respective German departments later had the possibility to establish their headquarters in the empty villas that had been owned by the Jews."

While admitting his own activities had overlapped the jurisdictions of other departments, Höttl attempted to step back from the noose of self-incrimination by telling the court how the lack of a central office had prevented him from being acquainted with all of the personnel dealing with the Jewish question. As a result, he had not been present when any of the defendants now in the dock, had openly discussed the deportations. That established, Höttl continued his portrait of the Nazi apparatus in Hungary with the focus now set on former SS General Otto Winkelmann.

Höttl: 1962

"For General Winkelmann, the assignment in Hungary was the fulfill-ment of his entire career. In my view he was a somewhat simple but very hu-morous police constable who wasn't prepared for the big political scene and all the intrigues that went along with it. On the other hand, Winkelmann was very ambitious to make his presence known and wanted again and again to make policy in Budapest."

Ironically, Winkelmann had levelled similar accusations at Höttl du-ring the trial of the Hungarian politician, Laszlo Baky, claiming that because of his strong ties to Kaltenbrunner, Höttl often felt free to dabble in freelan-ce politicking in Budapest. A clear example of that interference, according to Winkelmann, was Höttl's overt lobbying on behalf of Graf Fidel Palffy, leader of one of the Hungarian right-wing parties vying for power in the summer of 1944. Having failed in his attempts to have Palffy selected as a candidate to head the planned new government, Höttl reportedly managed to see Palffy appointed as Minister of Agriculture under Szalasi. During the same 1946 testimony, Winkelmann went on to state that although he didn't believe Höttl was directly involved in the measures against the Jews, he cer-tainly was aware of them. Sensing that comparable testimony might re-sur-face during the Krumey trial, Höttl tried to reduce the impact of any possib-le disclosures by subtly reminding the court it was Winkelmann who had been the head of the office responsible for the deportations.

Höttl: 1962

"Without doubt ,Winkelmann was officially responsible for establishing the necessary connections with the Hungarian departments, with someone of his rank. I am aware that Winkelmann had especially good relationships with both State Secretaries in the Interior Ministry, Dr. Laszlo Endre and Laszlo Baky. ... In any case, there were a number of early mornings meetings held regularly by Winkelmann at which individual functionaries from the various

German offices in Budapest attended. I also took part initially, though mainly to inform myself. Here, at least as long as I attended, it had mostly to do with military concerns and organizational problems, although commanders also brought up their intelligence suspicions. Later, concrete measures regarding the persecution of the Jews were the object of the discussions. But matters concerning the evacuation of the Jews were never discussed during my presence."

Willing to ignore what they knew to be half-truths, prosecutors directed their questions to who knew *'what'* and *'when'*.

Höttl: 1962
"When it is presented to me that certain of the accused operate from the claim that they were only aware of the deportations, and not the ultimate goal, namely the extermination, I can only say that in Budapest people in general spoke about where the deportations led, namely the extermination camps...I received official confirmation of such from Eichmann himself, where he openly admitted that those who were being arrested were going to be liquidated. As I said, man had long known about these liquidations, not least from someone who had escaped from a camp. That was reported on by the foreign stations which were not illegal to listen to in Hungary."

Despite their significant roles in the Hungarian tragedy, neither Veesenmayer nor Winkelmann suffered any severe consequences for their actions. Less than seven years after the end of the war both men were back in their respective civilian careers, able to live free from the threat of prosecution until passing away in 1977. Other leading figures involved in the Hungarian cataclysm met varying fates.

SS Capt. Franz Abromeit
An Eichmann advisor in both Croatia and Hungary, reportedly escaped to Egypt in 1945, before eventually being declared dead in 1964.

László Bardóssy, Andor Jaross, László Baky and László Endre
In early December 1944, the Hungarian provisional government in Debrecen began steps toward prosecuting suspected war criminals. One of the first to face the special courts, called *'people's* tribunals,' was former

Premier, László Bardossy, (1941-1942) Charged with complicity in the murder of Hungarian Jews at Kamenets – Podolski and Novi Sad, he was found guilty and hanged on January 10, 1946. Former Interior Minister, Andor Jaross, and his two undersecretaries, László Baky and László Endre, all three rabid anti-semites, were accused of having played major roles in the plundering and deportation of Hungarian Jewry. Convicted of their crimes, Baky and Endre were executed on March 26th. 1946. Found guilty in a separate trial, Jaross faced a firing squad on April 11th, 1946.

SS Colonel Kurt Becher

Sent to Budapest on a special economic contract to ostensibly obtain war materials for the Waffen SS, the well-known German businessman's assignment reportedly fell outside the jurisdiction of either the SS or police departments. Although he was not thought to have played a role in the Jewish deportations, he had been deeply involved in the confiscation and acquisition of Jewish properties.

Höttl: 1962

"Following the events of March 19, 1944 I met with Becher privately many times. Becher gave off the impression of having come from very good background. He had a refined manner and for this reason considered most of the functionaries working for the Third Reich in Hungary, especially in the police, as "proletariats". What is especially noteworthy in connection with my growing friendship with Becher was that he saw the war as lost for Germany. As is my nature, I made no secret of the fact that I had a negative opinion of the German foreign policy in general, and more so in Hungary. When Becher was aware of my thoughts, he also criticized many German measures in a straightforward manner. On one side Becher wanted to carry out his assignment, and on the other, didn't lose sight of the inevitable developments of the world political situation. I can't say with any certainty whether Becher's behaviour in Hungary was dictated by his emotional outlook or his clever foresight of the future collapse."

Höttl's fawning tone regarding Becher was indicative of the attitude a man from *"a family of limited means"* might demonstrate towards a successful and ambitious businessman. That said, his favourable comments may have also been tied to enduring rumours that all high-ranking SS officers had profited from Becher's dealings in Hungary. Captured by the Americans at the end of the war, Becher avoided having to face justice for his alleged actions, thanks in part to a letter of recommendation written for him by Rezno Kastner, a former member of the Jewish Rescue Committee. Once released, Becher returned to Germany, where he eventually rose to become head of his own grain and feed company in Bremen. He died a wealthy man in 1995, at the age of 85.

SS Capt. Theodor Dannecker

A former Eichmann aide active in anti-Jewish programs in Belgium, France, Bulgaria and Hungary, Dannecker was captured by the Americans and jailed in Bad Tölz. He was reported to have committed suicide on December 12th, 1945.

SS First Lt. Dr.Theodor Horst Grell

Arrested and held in Frankfurt am Main until investigations into his possible complicity were completed, Grell was released without being charged in July 1945. He was able to resume his law career until being re-arrested as part of the *'Wilhelmstrasse'* trial in 1947. Following the well-worn path of largely placing the blame on colleagues either dead or missing, Grell was released in August 1948, whereupon he moved to southern Bavaria to continue his law practice, occasionally interrupted by requests to testify at various trials.

Otto Hunsche

A former government advisor in the RSHA, Hunsche was arrested near Alt Aussee on May 12, 1945. After serving a light sentence, he moved to northern Germany in 1946 to resume his law career. One of many former henchmen re-arrested in the aftermath of Eichmann's capture, Hunsche was put on trial in a Frankfurt court in the mid 60's. Convicted in 1969, he was sentenced to 12 years.

Bela Imredy

Accused of having drafted and signed anti-Jewish Laws during his term as Hungarian Premier (1938-1939), documents which helped pave the way for later persecution, Imredy was put on trial on November 14, 1945. Found guilty, he was executed on March 1, 1946.

Rezno (Rudolph) Kasztner

Generally credited with having saved the lives of over 18,000 Jews, Kasztner moved to Israel after the war. Long viewed as a controversial figure, he was criticized for having testified on behalf of former Nazis at Nuremberg, in particular Kurt Becher. In response to the charge he collaborated with the Nazis, Kasztner filed a libel suit against the journalist Malkiel Grunwald in 1954. Kasztner lost the case, but before the Supreme Court could reach a verdict on his appeal, he was shot and killed by a national extremist in Tel Aviv on March 4th, 1957.

Baron Gabor Kemeny

Following his capture by American troops, the former Hungarian Foreign Minister was held in various POW camps in Italy before being returned to Budapest to stand trial with Szalasi. Convicted of the charges against him, he was ultimately hanged.

SS Lt. Colonel Hermann Krumey

Krumey was arrested in Italy in May 1945 and imprisoned until 1948, at which time an affidavit written by Rezno Kasztner helped facilitate his release. He returned to Germany to work as a pharmacist in the city of Korbach, before being rearrested in 1961. Tried and convicted, he was sentenced to five years hard labor. The prosecution however, appealed the sentence, forcing a second trial which ended in 1969 with a life sentence. Upheld by the German Federal Court in 1973, Krumey remained in prison until his death on Nov. 27, 1981.

SS Captain Franz Novak

After the war, Novak lived anonymously in Vienna, reportedly working as the manager of a printing shop. Able to regain his Austrian citizenship in 1957, the former transport co-ordinator was arrested in 1961, but released without being charged. Re-arrested in 1964, Novak was convicted but remained free on bail while the case was appealed. The series of appeals and re-trials would drag on for years and it wasn't until 1972 that Novak was finally sentenced to seven years for his involvement in the deportation of Hungarian Jews.

SS Capt. Dieter Wisliceny

Reportedly captured near Alt Aussee in 1945, the former deportation specialist for Greece and Hungary was extradited to Czechoslovakia to stand trial for his anti-Jewish activities in Slovakia. Convicted, he was hanged in Pressburg in 1948.

With regard to the central figure whose 'organizational talents' helped send millions to their death, Eichmann's fate was left in the hands of three Jerusalem judges once court proceedings ended on August 14th, 1961. After deliberating for nearly four months, on December 11th, the trio reached a guilty verdict on all counts. Four days later, Eichmann learned he was sentenced to die for his crimes. The defence filed an immediate appeal, but on May 29th, 1962 the Supreme Court of Israel rejected Eichmann's petition, stating *"We know only too well how utterly inadequate this death sentence is as compared to the millions of deaths in the most diverse ways inflicted on his victims."*

On the morning of May 31, 1962, languishing in his cell at Ramla prison, Eichmann awaited a decision on his final appeal to Israel President Ben-Zvi. All that day, the president received hundreds of telegrams and requests for leniency for the Nazi killer. Some people argued that executing Eichmann would merely be an act of revenge on the part of Israel, but President Ben-Zvi disagreed. In a brief statement to the press, he revealed his decision *"not to exercise his prerogative to pardon or reduce sentence in the case of Adolf Eichmann."*

At approximately 7 p.m., Eichmann was served his last meal. Fifty yards away, workers made final preparations to the gallows erected solely for his execution, reportedly the first ever built in Israel. Eichmann spoke with a Protestant minister until guards arrived to escort him. Once on the platform, his ankles and knees were tied together and his hands bound behind his back. Guards attempted to place a black hood over his head, but Eichmann refused. Unrepentant to the end, his final words were, *"Such is the fate of all men. Long live Germany, long live Argentina, long live Austria! I shall not forget them!"* Seconds after the noose was tightened around his neck, the trap door was sprung and Eichmann fell to his death. Following an examination by a government physician, he was pronounced dead at 23:58 hours. Shortly thereafter Israeli officials issued a statement acknowledging, *"Adolf Eichmann was executed by hanging today in accordance with the sentence of death passed by the Jerusalem District Court on December 15, 1961"* One hour later, his remains were cremated, placed aboard a police boat, and taken out beyond Israeli territorial waters, where at 3:45 am they were scattered into the dark waters of the Mediterranean.

By the summer of 1962, the scourge of unwanted publicity stirred up by various court proceedings had been hovering over Höttl for nearly two years. Despite the defiance or indifference he displayed in the wake of those events, those closest to Höttl knew he was often at pains to maintain a semblance of equilibrium in his daily life.

Andrea Hofer: (Höttl) 2002
"My mother claimed that he had always been a very nervous person."

One of the ways Höttl attempted to escape the media onslaught was to retreat into the Ausseerland landscape. During this period, he was often sighted on one of the trails that cut through the adjacent forests, or out for a walk around the lake, using the time to reflect on how he might shore up his teetering enterprise. One person often privy to those deliberations when home on semester breaks from his studies in Vienna, was Höttl's son, Völker. Having already deferred to his father's wishes to study History and Psychology rather than his own favoured Mathematics, Völker was frequently subjected to lectures on the importance of preserving the family legacy. Nonetheless, he made it clear to his father he had no interest in one day taking over administration of the school.

Andrea Hofer:(Höttl) 2002
"He was not a simple person. ... but he was of the opinion that children were there to obey. It was like that in many families, but he was perhaps extreme... he was of the opinion that everyone should align themselves according to his wishes."

Disturbed by his son's muted rebellion, as well as the worsening prospects for the school, Höttl occasionally sought refuge amongst his oldest and trusted cronies. Having never attained a driver's license, he had to rely on the services of Heinz Reith, a custodian at the school, whenever he felt the need to ease his *"beleaguered"* psyche with an evening of conversation at the Hotel Sonne's *"Stammtisch"* in Bad Aussee.

Meanwhile in Vienna, despite having declined the Hungarian request for Höttl's extradition, Austrian officials were working with district court officials in the State of Steiermark, to explore ways of bringing him to justice *domestically*. State attorneys in the city of Leoben, some 120 kilometres south east of Alt Aussee, had spent the better part of a year gathering evidence and by the fall of 1962, had mustered enough material to inform their fellow landsman he was once again under formal investigation. That had been no easy achievement. Options to prosecute suspected war criminals had been limited by the General Amnesty granted by the Austrian Federal President in 1952, which prohibited persons being placed back in the dock on charges they'd already faced. State authorities in Graz had also reminded their Leoben colleagues that previous domestic attempts to prosecute Höttl had all ended in failure. If those weren't deterrents enough, a recent study had concluded that large sections of previous testimony given in the immediate post-war years, had been self-serving, aimed at either shedding personal guilt or laying the groundwork for a rehabilitation. Amongst that *'tainted'* batch were the statements of Edmund Veesenmayer and Otto Winklemann.

Unintimidated by the uphill battle they were facing, Leoben officials announced plans to *"re-interview"* the two men regarding their knowledge of what by now had become the standard accusation against Höttl, having prepared lists of the regime's opponents. Arrangements were made for Veesenmayer and Winkelmann to testify from their respective home cities of Darmstadt and Bordesholm. Whether uninformed or simply unconcerned by the incriminating material Höttl had delivered about them during the Krumey trial, both men proceeded to back Höttl's assertions of having only been involved in peripheral intelligence work. Aware this 'new testimony' would not substantiate the *'list'* allegations, prosecutors shifted to a second charge Höttl had been arraigned on, namely that of larceny. This charge stemmed from the alleged misappropriation of valuable objects belonging to one Lajos Schulhoff, a Budapest Jew whose house had been located at Disz-Platz 7. Schulhoff had filed a similar suit against Höttl in Budapest in 1946, explaining how his household had been confiscated by the SS in March 1944, following his arrest and internment at a camp in Kistarcsa. Documents indicated the villa had been subsequently turned over to Höttl to serve as both his residence and office space for his staff. Circumstances had remained unchanged until late fall of '44 , when a general evacuation was instigated to retreat from the advancing Soviet army. As part of that process, Höttl and several SS accomplices had been observed removing the bulk of the villa's household furnishings and loading them on to several waiting trucks. Amongst the articles Schulhoff's caretaker, Joseph Toth, and his wife claimed to have seen taken, was a collection of valuable Turkish rugs, two engravings by the German artist Albert Dürer, a pair of pen and ink drawings by Mihaly Zichy, a series of framed engravings, as well as several oil paintings from other well known artists. In total Toth claimed twenty-seven crates had been hauled away, purported to have contained furniture, porcelain, china, and other valuable objects pilfered from neighbouring houses. Schulhoff had reported the theft to the Hungarian Foreign Ministry immediately after his return to Budapest. Hungarian officials had in turn requested authorities in Nuremberg to question Höttl about the incident. According to Schulhoff's affidavit, there had been no response to the entreaty. All further attempts at retribution had been abandoned until 1954 when Schulhoff wrote directly to Höttl. In a response issued several weeks later, Höttl denied any knowledge of the alleged theft. The matter was left in abeyance until 1961, when material from the Hungarian extradition request was passed on to Leoben officials.

Hoping to avoid another case of *"Aussage gegen Aussage"*, Leoben officials sought out other sources for information on the possible whereabouts of the stolen goods. One item of interest emerged from former Austrian Resistance fighter, Edith Frischmuth, who told investigators it was common knowledge amongst local residents, that Höttl had returned to Alt Aussee in late 1944, loaded down with *"material possessions taken from Hungary"*. Although Frischmuth was unable to provide specific evidence to back her statement, an obscure entry in the 1960 Austrian edition of *"Who's who"*, added credibility to her claim, by describing Höttl as an avid collector of art objects said to have included antique engravings, rugs and old prints. Thirty five years later, Frischmuth's remarks were strengthened further by an Alt Aussee resident's comment on Höttl's behaviour during tight financial times.

Berta Auerbach: Dec. 1997
"He must have run out of money for he was now selling carpets and paintings to make ends meet."

Early on in their investigation, Leoben prosecutors had also briefly considered adding a third charge to Höttl's roster, the spark for which arose from documents sent to them by the prosecutor's office in Düsseldorf. According to those reports, Höttl had been requested to testify earlier in 1962, in regards to the murder of State Secretary Freiherr von Ketteler on June 30th 1938. The victim had been serving as an attaché at the German Embassy in Vienna when it was discovered he was a member of a Catholic Resistance Organization. Rumours implied that plans for his murder had been conceived under the auspices of RSHA chief, Reinhard Heydrich. Having been a prominent figure in the Vienna SD with close ties to the RSHA in Berlin, Höttl was suspected of having had vital information about the murder. After conducting a review of Höttl's testimony however, Leoben officials felt there wasn't sufficient evidence to warrant a charge being included in the indictment.

In spite of all their initial optimism, in the end, Leoben prosecutors were no more successful than their predecessors. On February 13th, 1963, the District State attorney announced the entire proceedings were being dismissed due to insufficient evidence. Exonerated without having to appear in court, Höttl had once again slipped through judicial ropes seeking to bind him.

By the spring of 1963, cracks that had been visible in the school's faca-de for months, were rapidly approaching critical mass. Prompted by con-cerns Höttl had been juggling payments on old debts through the acquisiti-on of new loans, justice officials in Bad Aussee launched an investigation on behalf of many small merchants and banks to whom money was owed. (Volkstimme, 28.3.63) They soon discovered the school was in debt to the tune of some fifteen million Schillings. Despite earlier suspicions the school was in trouble, action had been delayed by the fact it was such a strong eco-nomic factor within the community. No one locally wanted to be seen as having initiated its demise. Such concerns however, carried little weight with Education officials in Vienna, where added to the inventory of other irregularities over the years, accusations of financial mismanagement were proving to be the last straw. Stipulating that administrative and academic standards were drastically in need of improvement, in May, Ministry offici-als informed Höttl of their intention to revoke the school's examining licen-se, adding there would be no chance of re-certification until changes were implemented. Although the decree was not to affect those students eligible to receive their *"Middle school"* diploma that semester, Höttl knew that wi-thout the opportunity to obtain their Matura in the future, students seeking a higher education would simply select other venues. A smaller exodus had already taken place due to restrictions imposed in 1961. By the time the se-cond decree was announced two years later, enrolment had plunged to a mere 138 students. News of the Ministry's latest ruling spread quickly th-roughout the community. Hoping to reduce speculation, officials made a point of listing a host of justifications for their action, but it wasn't long be-fore accusations began to surface the decision had been purely political.

Fr. Hofer (Höttl): 2002
"For reasons unknown to me, Dr. Drimmel had unleashed a personal crusade against my father... which culminated in the loss of the official license."

The man Frau Hofer accused of campaigning against her father was Dr. Heinrich Drimmel, Minister of Education in the ÖVP Cabinet of Aust-rian Chancellor Julius Raab. Drimmel's career in the field of education had been a lengthy one. After spending a sizeable portion of his youth in various Catholic groups, Drimmel went on to serve as head of the Austrian Universities Student Association while studying at the University of Vienna. He was elected President of the Catholic University Association in 1933, and following his graduation that year, began working for the Federal Finance Administration in Vienna. Transferred to the Education Ministry shortly thereafter, he continued his studies part time, obtaining his law degree in 1935. Dismissed by the Nazi administration in March 1938, Drimmel saw service on both eastern and south-eastern fronts before being captured in 1944. After 18 months in a prisoner of war camp, he returned to Vienna in late 1946 to resume work at the Ministry of Education. Promoted to the head offices of the Education Minister in 1947, he remained in that position until being named deputy Department Head of the Universities section in 1952. Two years later, his political career reached its zenith when Chancellor Raab appointed him Education Minister, a post he held for almost ten years before moving to the State Senate in April 1964.

Although there was no record of any personal acrimony between Höttl and Drimmel, speculation loomed that something in their shared past had played a role in the Ministry's annulment of the ÖR. Höttl attempted to use the spectre of a private vendetta by drawing attention to what he called his own *"connection"* to Austrian Chancellor Julius Raab, implying that Drimmel had been held in check until Raab's resignation in April 1961.

Höttl: 1999

"Herr Raab used to spend his summers and Christmas in Bad Aussee, and I was… not really friends but was a good acquaintance. In any case, Herr Raab thought highly of me and when he wanted to know something, he called me from the Chancellor's office in Vienna, and asked 'what do you say about this?' Or when he was here we would go for walks. He was a very underrated man because he was a simple man, and spoke with a dialect. The people who weren't close to him or didn't know him weren't aware of how clever he was or how competent. He was certainly the best politician we had from this circle… I have several photos taken with him and his sister."

Whether Höttl's embellished depiction of Raab as a departed protector had any substance or not, it is doubtful Drimmel's action in revoking the ÖR was taken unilaterally. More to the point was that Höttl had finally come to be seen as a political embarrassment by many in the government. Particularly grating for education officials was having to explain how and why a former SS officer and SD operative, wanted for war crimes in Hungary, had secured a forum from which he could significantly influence the schooling of Austrian youth.

Well acquainted with being *'maligned'* by those he labelled as foes, Höttl's response to the Ministry's order was to file a protest with the High Administrative Court of Austria. He knew there was little chance of the court's reinstating the ÖR any time soon, but felt a display of defiance was an integral part of the strategy to get public opinion behind him. Höttl also believed the process of building such support had to run parallel to reassuring critics and creditors the school was still a viable enterprise. Attending a town council meeting in Bad Aussee on May 18th, 1963, he insisted some sort of intervention be undertaken, warning councillors that 80% of the employees at the *'business'*, as he often called it, would be unemployed and the region dealt a severe economic blow if the school closed. On previous occasions the council had succumbed to such scare tactics, but this time Mayor Ludwig Viertbauer chose to rebuff Höttl's ultimatum. Closing ranks around their chairman, the town council passed a resolution instructing that no operating funds be made available unless the school became a separate entity from the Internat, and improvements were instituted in its academic and economic standards. Also included in the motion was the recommendation Höttl be replaced by someone with the confidence of the Ministry, one who would not interfere with the setting of the curriculum. A day after the council's resolution was made public, Deputy Mayor Lewandowski offered a candid description of their negotiating partner.

Deputy Mayor Lewandowski: (Volksstimme)
"......the old despot, who in every position he held during his time in the Third Reich, would climb over corpses in pursuit of what he wanted. He does what he wants. He sides with red as well as with black, wherever there is an advantage for him".

Already taken aback by the council's rejection, Höttl received a further blow to his pride when it was revealed the council had secretly backed the Ministry's decision to withdraw the school's certification. (Neue Österreich) Clearly no longer able to intimidate town officials, Höttl retaliated by reaching out directly to the community itself. As the battle lines formed, it quickly became apparent how multi-layered Höttl's array of contacts and influences had become. Amongst the prominent citizens mobilized to speak on his behalf, were Graf Marenzi and Dr. Umlauf, two federally elected representatives that had apparently intervened in his favour on prior instances at the Ministry in Vienna. In addition to these individuals, Steiermark state politician Josef Krainer, as well as several members of the Federal Parliament, Herrn Rainer, Prinke and Rehor, displayed a willingness to assist, either through timely telephone calls, informal discussions or the formation of spontaneous committees. According to one report, Minister Drimmel himself came under pressure from influential parents, likely exhorted by Höttl's dire predictions that graduation could not be assured if present circumstances prevailed. As the concerted propaganda blitz continued over the next few months, Höttl quietly sought a back door way of reaching a negotiated compromise. At some point in the late summer of 1963, an interim settlement was achieved with local and State officials, calling for the addition of several new subjects to the curriculum, as well as assurance that all teachers would undergo appropriate aptitude tests. The most bitter pill to swallow was the codicil that as administrator, Höttl would no longer attempt to exert unauthorized influence on either the school director or any of the teachers. Despite the fact the school could only regain its certification if and when all demands of the settlement were met, Höttl appeared in no rush to actualize its *"cumbersome"* edicts.

The tentative agreement had still not been fully implemented by the time the High Court decision on Höttl's appeal was handed down in December. Although the court found evidence of considerable *"irregularities"* at the school, it judged Höttl had been justified in disputing the assertions against him. As a result, it ordered the Ministry of Education to conduct a comprehensive review of its decision to annul the ÖR. (Volksstimme 17.12.1963) Höttl was initially buoyed by the temporary reprieve, convinced the normal slow pace of reviews would provide extra time to find a solution. Two weeks later, his plans suffered a setback when Ministry officials dispatched a response confirming the earlier judgement had been warranted, re-emphasizing that if the school were allowed to retain its official authority with its current standard of teaching methods, the quality of education would remain diminished and the potential for improprieties enhanced.

One month later, Höttl filed for the school's bankruptcy. In a gesture befitting a consummate opportunist, prior to submitting the required documents, he allegedly transferred his own personal investments out of the school, thereby placing them beyond the reach of bank investigators. Capitalizing on the bankruptcy laws in existence at the time, he also managed to salvage a portion of his empire under the new title of Private Maturaschule GmbH.Bad Aussee. Although he was required to relinquish the other portions of his enterprise, the negotiated deal allowed him to maintain a twenty-five percent interest in the newly created institution. The remaining equity was to be shared by creditors and the State of Steiermark. Heralded as an exclusive boarding school, tailored to educate and prepare students for their Matura in Vienna, the company was to be located in Schloss Ramgut, the only building to escape confiscation by the bankruptcy court.

Despite his measured success, Höttl found it difficult to hide his rancour at the loss of the old school to the State School Board. To make matters worse, the directorship of the old school was once again placed in the hands of Dr. Gunther Legat, the very man Höttl felt had played a pivotal role in its decline. Added to Höttl's chagrin was the fact that through Legat's efforts the school eventually succeeded in regaining its ÖR status in 1965. Thirty years later, in an aside to an Alt Aussee resident, Höttl admitted that one of his greatest disappointments in life, remained his failure to retrieve the official certification for 'mein Schule'.

In the weeks leading up to the loss of his school, Höttl had continued to be hounded by assorted legal difficulties. No sooner had the favourable ruling by the High Court been delivered, he was handed notice another Austrian court intended to investigate him, this time in regards to a charge of perjury. Initiated by a Berlin journalist named Julius Mader, one of many reporters to have publicized Höttl's wartime activities as part of their coverage of the Eichmann trial, the deposition claimed certain statements in Höttl's testimony for that trial contravened Austrian perjury laws. More specifically, Mader claimed Höttl had been an active member of the SS and SD much earlier than he purported, and that his involvement in the Arrow Cross putsch in October 1944 had been misleading. Support for the latter claim was supplied by Hungarian journalists Istvan Pinter and Laszlo Szabo, in their book, 'The Unpunished War Criminals'.

Pinter/Szabo:

"It was Dr. Höttl who encouraged the Cross Fire people. He allowed Kovarcz to be brought back to Hungary. Emil Kovarcz, had fled Budapest before the German entry after he was suspected of murdering two Socialist journalists. After re-entering the country he had become deeply involved in the preparation of the putsch and was rewarded with an important position in Szalasi's Government). Last, but not least, it was Höttl's reports to Himmler and Hitler that helped them decide in favour of the Cross Fire. The Szalasi people didn't declare Höttl to be a persona non grata, rather the opposite, they awarded him with a high decoration."

Supplementing Mader's allegations was a document signed by the Hungarian Fascist President, Ferenc Szalasi. Dated December 1st 1944, it held a list of seventeen people who were to be awarded the Officer's Cross of the Holy Hungarian Crown for their service in the Arrow Cross putsch. The seventh name on the list was that of Wilhelm Höttl.

Following a preliminary examination of the evidence, State officials referred the case to the district court in Leoben. Still smarting from their previous defeat, investigators there nonetheless agreed to re-examine Höttl's statements from the Eichmann and Krumey trials. Despite the fact the *"award list"* appeared to provide conclusive evidence of perjury on

Höttl's part, Leoben officials later dispatched a memo to State prosecutors in Graz, advising that based on their findings, there seemed little chance of conviction. To Höttl's fortune, authorities in Graz chose to accept the recommendation and on March 11th, 1964, dismissed the proceedings, making the Mader process the last court challenge Höttl would face for nearly a decade.

With the tumult of the Eichmann trial, assorted court appearances, and the loss of his *'beloved'* school behind him, Höttl once again withdrew into the relative obscurity of an *'unassuming'* lifestyle. Aside from his limited duties at the Internat, much of his time was again spent walking in the forest, occasionally followed by curious schoolchildren convinced he was off to retrieve pieces of a buried treasure. It was while on one of these lengthy excursions, the idea of fashioning a career as *"Zeitzeuge"* (witness to the times) began to take shape. The publication of two books had shown Höttl the financial gains to be made from catering to the unrelenting interest in Nazi folklore, as had an interview given to the Hungarian-born journalist, Ladislas Faragó in 1953. Having been an agent in both Turkey and Hungary during the war, Faragó was no stranger to the world of espionage, and keenly aware of the profits to be made from marketing oneself as an *'insider'*. Höttl was impressed enough by the subsequent success of Faragó's article, to try his own hand in the field. His story, modestly titled *"I was Hitler's Master Spy, was published in the November issue of Argosy magazine in 1953. Portraying himself as a* "marked man, hunted and harassed", he recounted his life since the close of the war as having been full of strangers and secret agents, charged with the sole intention of observing and entrapping him. Dismissed at the time as the bluster of a last hurrah, the venture nonetheless served as proof of the viability of dispensing his memories for cash. While familial and administrative obligations may have precluded his becoming an *'authoritative'* consultant throughout much of the 50's and 60's, recent developments had reduced those commitments to such an extent, that Höttl now had the freedom to transform himself into a saleable 'chronicler of the times'.

Höttl: 1999
"Those who cannot recognize or accept that their 'days of glory' are gone, have a difficult time in life."

Völker Höttl: 2001

"He managed to achieve what many others in Austria today have yet to achieve......At some point he recognized that many things he had done had been wrong, and he began to view the period from the perspective of a historian, and not as someone who had participated in it, helped guide it and gone along with it. At some point he said "this one theme is over for me, today I am an historian. Anyone can approach me, I am an historian and a witness. This combination was always important for him."

How authentic Höttl's shift in thinking truly was and what impact it had on his approach to documenting the past is debatable. He had after all, long been recognized by family and friends, not to mention a legion of investigators, as someone who could suppress or adjust facts at will.

Völker Höttl: 2001

"Let's put it this way, in the beginning the truth was surely sparse and then only what was necessary. As he got older and there was more distance between that period and the present, the more neutrally the period was seen, then he was quite open."

Höttl's efforts to develop into a historiographer got underway in earnest in 1964, and he was able to avail himself of nearly an eight year unhindered run towards that quest until 1972, when a summons to testify at the trial of former Hamburg Gestapo Chief, SS Major General Bruno Heinrich Streckenbach arrived on his doorstep. As on previous occasions, arrangements were made for him to deliver his testimony from Bad Aussee. After updating the routine protocol, this time as 57 year old, married Roman Catholic, Höttl launched into a brief synopsis of his own career, accompanied by the usual distortions. When questioning turned to more specific knowledge of Streckenbach's powers and activities, he told prosecutors that as head of Amt I, (Personnel) at the RSHA, Streckenbach, had wielded an inordinate amount of influence over other departments, influence that was especially pronounced when it came to the evolution of the notorious Einsatzgruppen. According to Höttl, the idea for the Einsatzgruppen had originated from Heydrich, but it was Streckenbach, who had carried out the directives with conviction and brutality, often assigning people to the special killing units as a way of getting rid of them. One of the victim's of that unrestricted authority had been Höttl's old mentor, Brigadier Gen. Heinz Jost, who was transferred to one of the Einsatzgruppen at Streckenbach's insistence in early 1942. As gratified as Höttl may have been for the opportunity to settle the score on Jost's behalf, his testimony did not appear to play a big role in the outcome of the trial. Despite having been charged with the deaths of over one million people, the proceedings against Streckenbach were stayed in 1974 due to his purported poor health. Despite that diagnosis, Streckenbach managed to live another three years, before dying in Hamburg in October 1977.

As innocuous as Höttl's testimony may have appeared to many observers, it did not prevent the burgeoning historian from continuing to disseminate further wisdoms, especially if there was a fee involved. One such example was an interview given to the German Newspaper, 'Die Welt' in the early 70's. More or less a revised version of the 'My friend Eichmann' missive written in the 60's, it thrust Höttl back into the media spotlight.

Völker Höttl: 2001
"He had something in the interview that had been blown up and after that he was naturally more cautious with what he said."

Although the luminescence created by the 'Die Welt' article proved temporary, it was enough to prompt Höttl to be slightly more selective about his choice of audiences. But with no further lawsuits, court appearances, or scandals to encumber him, Höttl was free to spend the remainder of the decade indulging in the heady and lucrative world of historiography, meeting and greeting students, amateur historians, archivists, and television producers who continued to flock to Alt Aussee for his rendition of the past.

Despite the bleak future the Internat had faced in 1964, the institute could take credit for having prepared hundreds of students for their Matura during its fifteen years under Höttl's guidance. In a chapter devoted to the school in his final memoir, 'Einsatz für das Reich', Höttl described how problems began in the late 70's, when the previous owner of Schloss Ramgut surfaced and proceeded to reclaim the premises room by room, ostensibly to free up space for his own furniture collection. Other sources claimed the circumstances behind the school's decline were more complicated and ignominious than those alluded to in his book. Recalling her father's efforts to save the school, Andrea Hofer spoke of his having approached a large Internat near Vienna with the suggestion the Bad Aussee Maturaschule be purchased and run as a subsidiary. Maturaschule in general had grown in popularity since the mid 1960's, but the idea of amalgamating Höttl's school generated little enthusiasm in Vienna. The reluctance was particularly curious given that other than needing new residential facilities,the Internat was still a viable prospect. With no clear buyer in sight and dwindling income caused by the reduction in student living quarters, uncertainty over the school's future continued to put pressure on Höttl. Unable to produce a last minute solution, in 1980, Höttl decided to close the school once and for all rather than see it slide into insolvency.

From all appearances, Höttl's exit from the academic stage was not a graceful one. Six months after formally vacating Schloss Ramgut, he was named in a lawsuit charging him, his wife, and a third person with grand theft. According to an article in the Austrian newspaper, Kleine Zeitung on August 1st, 1995, the original owner, Baron Oppenheimer, had returned to the villa after Höttl's departure to discover a number of valuable items missing. The loss was reported to authorities but a subsequent search of Höttl's residence failed to turn up any incriminating evidence. Seeking 500,000 Schillings in damages, the suit claimed a Renaissance chair, a silver Rococo soup tureen, and a Pinzgauer wooden bed from the year 1768, had been amongst the items Höttl and his associates were alleged to have stolen and sold to cover the construction of his new home. Höttl protested his innocence vehemently, claiming the charges were simply a matter of intrigue and that Oppenheimer had previously agreed to his 'selecting' various pieces stored at the villa as compensation for renovations carried out since taking occupation in 1959. Joining the fray, Elfriede Höttl, insisted the charges were an act of revenge by a woman who had acted as a real esate agent between the Höttls and Oppenheimer, a woman who in her words *"was always hot for my man"*.

Despite what was rapidly shaping up to be yet another case of 'Aussage gegen Aussage', Höttl was nonetheless summoned to attend the district court in Leoben. After initially ignoring a number of petitions for his client to appear, Höttl's lawyer issued a statement to court officials claiming he was too ill to travel due to vascular obstructions and heart flutter. Whether due to Höttl's alleged poor health or not, like so many others that had preceded it, the case seems to have just faded from the radar.

Approximately fifteen years later, a prosecuting attorney in Leoben by the name of Dr. Andreas Haidacher decided to re-open the case. Well acquainted with Höttl's tendency to develop a serious illness whenever a court appearance loomed, Haidacher took the precaution of assigning a Graz based doctor to examine him six months prior to the planned litigation. As part of the standard protocol, the doctor closely reviewed reports from previous examinations before travelling to Alt Aussee. In carrying out the review, the doctor noted that Höttl's excusal from a courtroom in 1990, had been due to a series of diagnosed maladies. Those had included damaged heart muscle with indications of decompensation, obstruction in the intestinal tract, and a small cancerous growth on his face. A second report from April 1994, showed Höttl's having undergone several operations, one to remove a suspected intestinal tumour, one on his prostrate, and another on his left eye. Although the report suggested he had sufficiently recovered from the surgeries to attend trial, a follow-up examination four months later cast doubt on that assessment by revealing Höttl was also suffering from chronic heart failure, Parkinson's, and fat metabolic disorder. As a result of his review, the doctor half expected to see a man at death's door when he visited Höttl's residence on April 8th, 1995.

Unlike earlier assessments which had largely concentrated on physical ailments, the examination that day also included an appraisal of the 80 year old's mental state. Noting Höttl's 'critical awareness', the doctor later made mention of his tendency to display an air of superiority and strong need for acknowledgement. He also recorded that Höttl gave the impression of being in a general state of depressiveness, (later presumed due to his wife's severe illness), concluding his appraisal by stating the patient's intellectual and comprehension capacities appeared to be fully operative. The doctor's conclusions were forwarded to Haidacher in early May. Taken together with previous reports, the medical findings appeared to be grounds for a postponement, if not outright adjournment of the case. Before his lawyer could table such a motion, Höttl surprised his adversaries by agreeing to appear in June or July, provided arrangements were made for the care of Elfriede, who by this time was suffering from diabetes and recurring bouts of Parkinson's.

Following a series of delays, the hearing was finally scheduled to begin in Bad Aussee in October 1995. As the proceedings got underway, prosecutors were stunned to learn that in the interim, the Statute of Limitations had expired on several of the original charges. Plowing ahead with the remnants of their strategy nevertheless, Haidacher watched as the hearing stumbled through a string of interruptions over the next few weeks, including one caused by a torn Achilles tendon Höttl sustained on a walk in November. Ultimately unable to introduce enough evidence to make the remaining charges stick, the case was dismissed without a verdict in June of 1997.

In what was destined to be the final decade of Höttl's life, many of the roles he had assumed since the end of the war continued to serve him well. Adaptable versions of guilt and blame that had been erected in the late 40's, modified in the 50's, and dispensed in the 60's and 70's, hit full stride in the late 1980's, as those in search of his sagacity made the trek to Alt Aussee. Despite the threadbare tales often collected for their time and money, Höttl's reputation remained remarkably intact. Rarely one to shy away from saluting his successes, Höttl credited his achievements as a historiographer to his considerable 'experience' and ability to articulate it. What he neglected to mention was that his 'accomplishments' in the field had been just as much influenced by the fates of many of his former associates. Death, exile, and a timorousness born of lengthy prison terms had made numerous colleagues unable or reluctant to verbalize their past exploits, thereby reducing the competition Höttl faced as a 'Zeitzeuge'. Another factor in Höttl's 'success' was that many, if not most of those who genuinely regretted their roles during the Nazi era, either remained silent or went largely unnoticed. As a result of these various factors, Höttl's reputation as an articulate, albeit somewhat predictable purveyor of Nazi lore grew proportionately.

Völker Höttl: 2001
"Yes, he enjoyed doing that. Even if a week earlier he had been ill and had laid in bed. If somebody phoned, he was suddenly fit again and could give an interview for hours. He was quite open when students came from Vienna, but after everything he'd been through, he didn't want to offer his views to the press or to the public. With the foreign television networks, like the BBC he was also quite open, but like I said, that developed over a period of time."

Having paid substantial sums to rent access to Höttl's memory bank, a good number of journalists chose not to confront him over obvious discrepancies in his remarks. Fortunately, that approach was not universal and occasionally a well-researched reporter was able to jar Höttl out of his pre-packaged monologue with interesting results. One such encounter occurred when he was asked about the entry in the 1960 edition of *"Who's Who in Austria"* which had listed him as a collector of antique engravings and old prints. First allowing him to wax eloquently about the pleasures derived from his purported collection, the journalist turned to the question of its source, citing the lawsuit instituted in Budapest. Met with an expected refutation of the lawsuit's legitimacy, the journalist drew Höttl's attention to testimony in which he had claimed to have financed a portion of his school through the sale of a number of antiques, including rugs, jewelry and photo equipment, all purportedly purchased with the $700 monthly salary earned while with the CIC. As on previous occasions when he found himself confronted by circumstances he felt impugned his integrity, Höttl simply reverted to the old tactic of smugly dismissing the 'myths' with a series of smirks and shrugs. Over the years, the strategy proved effective in deterring guests from further probing, which they knew could provoke Höttl to either veer off into inconsequential anecdotes, or issue subtle threats to bring the interview to an end.

For the most part, Höttl preferred to dole out his bales of wisdom from the confines of his home. Experience had taught him there was considerably less control over the tone and flow of discussions when engaged outside the frame of formal interviews. One publicized assault, which threatened to damage his persona as a bonafide witness to the times, stemmed from the remarks of a fellow Austrian by the name of Gerd Honsik.

Born in 1941, Honsik had led a rather colourful career, if one can define multiple shades of brown as being colourful, before settling down to express his version of war-time events in a book called 'Freispruch fur Hitler', a title so absurd it deserves no translation. Prior to embarking on this epic, Honsik had reportedly consulted a number of 'experts', hoping to gather support for his theories. Two of those quoted at length were Höttl's old friend, Erich Kernmayer and his old nemesis, Otto Skorzeny. As portions of Höttl's own purveyed recollections happened to conflict strongly with Honsik's own vision of history, the latter felt compelled to call upon his countryman to renounce his erroneous statements. The thrust of Honsik's rebuke revolved around testimony given at Nuremberg, specifically in reference to Eichmann's figure of six million. Normally Höttl's response to aspersions from revisionists looking to further their own agendas was simply to ignore them, and in Honsik's case that is exactly what he did. In the mid 90's however, a particularly vitriolic letter from an unnamed woman in Graz, forced him to adapt that strategy. The letter in question implored him to grasp the chance to retract the 'horrendous injustice' he had committed against the German people at Nuremberg, describing his offence as being of incalculable consequence, and one which had resulted in students being dragged into concentration camp museums and shown facilities that were never used as gas chambers. The author also accused Höttl of having supplied information that eventually led to the jailing or execution of many former comrades. Only through a complete and honest confession, the woman wrote, could the lies of Nuremberg be exposed, and Höttl receive redemption. Intent on protecting his standing amongst remaining Nazis, as well as engaging in a bit of promotion for his reputation as a historiographer, Höttl delivered his retort in a letter to an Austrian reporter in April,1996.

Höttl: 1996

"Dear Frau _____

Since my return from American imprisonment at the end of 1947, I have received countless letters similar to yours accusing me of being a traitor. Although none were quite so foolish as yours, all demonstrated that the authors had not taken the trouble to study my explanation at Nuremberg... I never appeared there as a witness. Nor did I initiate the six million number, I just quoted what Eichmann had told me, in the assumption that he of all people must have known the number of murdered. That this wasn't correct, I have known for a long time but at least I have made the effort to research where it came from... You can read about all of that and more in my memoirs, that will be published in the fall of this year by a German publisher, who by the way is constantly in trouble because of its "rightist tendencies". .... In closing, a final question. How did you come to conclude that I wanted to "save my skin" with my explanation? My "crimes" consist solely of having been a Major in the SS, which made me guilty of being a member of a criminal organization. Are you also advocating collective guilt?

Yours truly,

W. Höttl. "

One year later, Höttl chose to expand his thoughts on the subject in a private interview.

Höttl: 1997

"On one side, for the true radical Nazis, or neo-Nazis, I was seen as a traitor. Some felt the Eichmann testimony had incriminated the entire

German people and all the National Socialists. On the other side, others felt that as an SS officer I was obligated to give some sort of an explanation. They weren't satisfied with me either. I first came into this crossfire with my books and then again with the Eichmann process. For some I was too much of a Nazi, for others not enough."

With the Graz letter still fresh in his mind, another example of that enduring dichotomy was about to surface, as one side of the divide suddenly deemed him worthy of official recognition.

On June 26, 1995, the State Government of Steiermark, announced its intention to award its Golden Service Cross to none other than Wilhelm Georg Höttl. Commending him for the *"courage to take a risk"* in founding his school in 1952, as well as for his numerous works as a historian, the deputy Governor, Dr. Peter Schachner-Blazizek, himself a former student at Höttl's school, informed his erstwhile director, the honour was to be bestowed in appreciation for his many years of exceptional work on behalf of his home state and its people. To put it mildly, Schachner-Blazizek's unexpected disclosure did not meet with the unanimous approval of the general populace. Within days, a firestorm of controversy erupted across the country. Articles protesting the government's intention to honour a former SS man, speculated on the motives Steiermark officials had in doing so. Bearing the brunt of the criticism was the Austrian People's Party's (ÖVP) State chairman, Dr. Josef Krainer. All but ignoring the torrent of admonishments, Krainer refused to back down, stating that as with all nominees, Höttl's *'police'* records had been checked and nothing found that would disqualify him from receiving the award. Such clarifications did little to quell the wave of criticism and indignation as editorials continued to castigate the government's insensitivity. Many political pundits were quick to point out such behaviour was to be expected from an area long stamped as a *"brown nest"*. Others suggested honouring Höttl was a subtle act of defiance, meant to counter the censuring Steiermark authorities had received a few months prior. According to this theory, officials in the State capital of Graz were still smarting from criticism over their dealings with a man named Herwig Nachtmann. As publisher of the rightist monthly magazine, Aula, Nachtmann had been charged with violating one of the country's anti-hate laws. The indictment stemmed from an article published in Aula in the summer of 1994, titled, 'Naturgesetze gelten für Nazis und Antifaschisten,' (The law of Nature applies to Nazis and anti-Fascists"). Although aimed primarily at Roma and Sinti, the article had also contained sections where NS crimes against humanity and mass gassings were minimized or in some cases even ridiculed. During the course of the proceedings against Nachtmann, attention was drawn to the fact that at the time of the article's publication, Aula had been benefitting from a number of generous contracts sent its way by Steiermark government officials. The disclosure subsequently led to demands State politicians disassociate themselves from the accused and the magazine, but few chose to comply. Taking the heat for that stance were State Chairman Josef Krainer and his deputy SPÖ-Vice Chairman, Peter Schachner-Blazizek. The insinuation was that having been angered by the criticism surrounding the Nachtmann case, the State government had decided in a unanimous vote, to exercise its authority, by awarding its highest honour to a former high ranking officer of the SS. Amongst the deluge of protests over that decision, was an earlier recipient of the Golden Service Cross named Albert Kaufmann. Kaufmann came forward to declare he did not wish to be included in the same company with SS man Höttl and threatened to return his medal if the award ceremony was carried out. In letters to the editors of various papers, former victims of Nazi aggression also complained bitterly at the mere prospect of Höttl being considered for such an award.

E. Schmidt, Graz: 1995
"It is an insult to all NS victims that 50 years after the liberation, such a 'traitor' is honoured with the highest award of the Province".

In addition to these gestures, a committee of surviving members of the Mauthausen concentration camp wrote to Krainer's office deploring the proposed award. Seemingly undeterred by the outcry, Krainer resolutely allowed preparations for the planned ceremony in Graz to continue.

Once again engulfed in the glare of publicity, this time Höttl reacted with uncharacteristic humility, limiting his remarks to a defence against some of the*"falsehoods"* he claimed were being perpetrated on his character. Despite all the previous diagnoses of being too ill to travel, on July 11th, Höttl stood before an audience of family, friends and invited guests in Graz, to officially receive the Golden Service Cross from the ÖVP leader.

Krainer and his colleagues may have successfully withstood pressure to abort plans to honour Höttl, but their success came at a cost. Criticism failed to abate following the ceremony, flaring even higher when it was revealed Höttl had kept silent about his past in the SS and SD, when submitting his curriculum to the nominating committee. Subsequent attempts to question members of the committee proved fruitless. One journalist spoke for many when he said, *"with the standards applied by the Steiermark, even Hitler would have been eligible".* (Neues Zeitung 21.7.1995)

Several weeks later, in what was viewed as a direct consequence to the medal debacle, the ruling SPÖ federal government in Vienna announced changes would be forthcoming in the methods of inspecting future award recipients. For Höttl himself, the continuing ballyhoo in the press and cafes quickly became ancient histrionics. With the medal safely stowed above the mantle in his living room, and his place in posterity assured, Höttl turned his focus towards what would be his final 'accomplishment.'

By the early 1990's, Höttl's status as a *"Zeitzeuge"* within the lucrative milieu of television documentaries had become well established. Considering that relative success, the question begs, why someone in his late seventies, would embark on the exhausting task of writing a third and final memoir. Some observers credited the Steiermark medal as having been the impetus to assure his *"rightful place"* in history, but the truth was that initial work on the book had begun almost ten years earlier. The genesis for what ultimately became the most lengthy and detailed, if not always accurate, of Höttl's literary efforts, appears to have emerged from his long-standing association with Dr. Peter Broucek, at the time an archivist at the National State Archives in Vienna. According to a series of letters exchanged between the two in the early 1980's, Höttl had become acquainted with Broucek while acting as an advisor on the archivist's project to edit the memoirs of Edmund Glaise Horstenau, memoirs Höttl at one time claimed to have written and smuggled out of the prison at Nuremberg. A close friendship gradually evolved between the two men through their co-operation on the Horstenau project, strengthened by the discovery Broucek's *"Uncle Emil"* was an old colleague of Höttl's from his student days at the University of Vienna. As the relationship deepened, Höttl began to share more and more of his own personal memories, admitting to having been the leader of the illegal SD in Vienna in the mid '30's, and referring to his close relationship with Ernst Kaltenbrunner. He also revealed how he had illegally photographed the scribbled diaries of Benito Mussolini before passing them on to his secretary, Hildegard Beetz for translation. (A section of the diaries would appear in the Appendix of Höttl's final book) In a letter to Broucek, dated Nov. 18th 1981, Höttl made the additional disclosure that while interned at Nuremberg, he had informed former German Chancellor, Franz von Papen, that a certain SS Colonel Böhme had been responsible for the murder of State Secretary Ketteler inn1938. According to Höttl, Böhme, later head of the SD in Böhmen, had held Ketteler's head under water until he drowned, information that Höttl had somehow been unable to recall for Düsseldorf prosecutors investigating the murder. As a result of the maturing trust between them, Höttl eventually decided to grant the archivist limited access to his vast trove of private papers. Broucek was overwhelmed by the size and content of the cache, and set out to convince Höttl it was his duty to history to share some of the sequestered material with the public. Despite Höttl's complaint that his *"old brain wasn't working as good as it used to"*, over the next few years, the pair made considerable progress in filtering the mass of information into a readable form. The first signs a manuscript had been completed came in an article in a local newspaper on December 23rd, 1996. Describing a reading Höttl had purportedly given at the Hotel Sonne in Bad Aussee, the article neglected to include an in-depth analysis of the excerpts, but did find it necessary to mention Höttl appeared to be in visible pain during the brief presentation. Despite the apparent illness, which turned out to be the after affects of a gall bladder colic, final editing of the manuscript continued until 'Einsatz für das Reich' was ready for publication.

Höttl: 1999

"The original title was "The Destroyed Dream of the Reich". I chose that title but my publisher decided to change it to something more interesting like the Foreign Intelligence Service, or In the Foreign Intelligence Service for the Reich. He thought that for sales of the book, "The Destroyed Dream of the Reich sounded too idealistic." In terms of potential, changing the name was certainly the right decision."

Sparring over the title was not the only discord encountered with his prospective publisher. A rigorous discussion had also taken place over the manner in which Höttl proposed the contents be presented.

Völker Höttl: 2001

"The publisher told him that they were interested in his memoirs, but he told them that he wanted to write as a historian. Basically he wanted it to be seen as he presented it. The publisher said that he couldn't write as a historian because he had been cut off from new information for decades. Some things can be viewed one way or the other, but they have all been examined endlessly... it's simply a matter of bringing new things to light. That's why he went over to Bublies... there he could write how he wanted."

Although Höttl succeeded in writing as he saw fit, the finished work failed to capture the attention or interest of the general reading public. Within months of its release, it was clear his final volume of narratives was unlikely to match the financial or critical success of its two predecessors.

Calling the book by and large *"stillborn"*, Völker Höttl surmised its fate was sealed even before publication by having *'mistakenly'* chosen a publishing house known for its right wing reputation. More objective critics viewed the book as nothing more than a product of, and for, the right wing spectrum. Others dismissed it as pure self-serving fantasy, refusing to even review it. Given that large portions of its 530 pages were sprinkled with questionable interpretations of known events, as well as dubious anecdotes such as the Vienna Boys Choir saga, the assessments appeared warranted. Despite its having fallen far short of expectations, Höttl did not seem greatly perturbed by the limited sales or lack of literary kudos. The book's muted reception also failed to affect his reputation as a *'Zeitzeuge'* or tarnish his status amongst many of the locals as sightings of Höttl savouring his customary quarter litre of white wine amongst a corral of old confidants remained a common occurrence.

Bad Aussee Store Manager: 1997
"Er ist eine gern gesehene Persönlichkeit, hier in diese Stadt. Wissen Sie, nicht alle SS Leute waren Mörderer." (He is highly welcomed personality in this town… You know, not all SS people were murderers".)

With their joint retirement in 1980, Wilhelm and Elfriede Höttl had been married for more than forty-two years. Despite claims from her children that she had always given in to her husband, throughout the years 'Friedl' had remained one of Höttl's closest confidants. Back as far as their days together at university, he had relied heavily on her judgement and advice to assist him through an assortment of difficult situations, situations which were especially acute when his later duties had imposed extended separations. During most of Höttl's long post-war internment, Elfriede had remained in Alt Aussee, keeping her family afloat with the aid of her parents, in- laws and friends, one of whom was Iris Scheidler, wife of Kaltenbrunner's former adjutant. In the closely monitored atmosphere of post-war Alt Aussee, such friendships quickly came to the attention of Allied officials stationed there. Suspecting their high-ranking husbands may have provided them access to privileged information, CIC officials reportedly approached both women with the prospect of becoming 'informants'. As conditions in Austria in general had been taxing at this time, both Höttl and Scheidler were rumoured to have agreed, hoping it would not only alleviate their own situations, but that of their jailed husbands as well. In their search for relevant information, American officials had also been seeking clues to the possible whereabouts of missing Nazi treasures. Their interest was heightened when the 34 four year old Scheidler reportedly supplied CIC officials with information that a part of the sought-after fortune was buried near the gates of the former prison sub-camp at Ebensee. Already under suspicion for having dealt illegally in gold, the Americans presumed Scheidler's information had come from her imprisoned husband. What they didn't know at the time was that Arthur Scheidler had intentionally planted a false tip, hoping to discredit his wife after learning of her plans to desert him for an American Colonel. Adding to the confusion was a rumour that Elfriede had recently informed a local policeman and CIC operative that the bulk of the missing gold was to be found on the Blaa Alm. Hoping to shed more light on that claim, in April 1947, Elfriede had been briefly transferred to Vienna for more questioning. Despite having allegedly provided additional information on the location of gold missing from the Russian Church, as well as a story of Himmler's gold-laden car having been sunk in the lake at Zell am See, none of the tips offered by the women led to any discoveries.

Andrea Hofer: 2003

"I can't say if all that is true or false. In 1947, Völker was 5 years and I, two. It would be possible that my mother and Iris Scheidler thought they were able to help her husbands. My mother never told us anything about this time but I can't believe that she knew something about Nazi treasure. If she had why wouldn't my parents have had more money in the years after the war? Why did the school go bankrupt? When my father died, there was no money to inherit. We never had a lifestyle with a lot of money."

Three and a half decades later, with or without access to a missing treasure, Elfriede had been looking forward to a retirement where she could devote her time and attention to a number of leisure-oriented activities. By 1987 however, the first of what would become a series of debilitating illnesses surfaced. Writing to a friend that same year, Höttl revealed his wife had been diagnosed with the onset of Parkinson's. Diabetes followed two years later, and for the next ten years a good portion of Elfriede's life was spent in and out of various clinics. Statements attributed to her during this period also raised questions as to how much her illnesses were affecting her mental capacities.

Elfriede Höttl: 1990's

"My husband and I had always disliked the Nazis."
(Nazi Millionaires book).

Elfriede may have experienced a number of mutations throughout her lifetime, but being an opponent of the Nazis had never been one of them. As an example of her flexibility, prior to 1938, she had considered herself to be a *"Gottgläubig"* Catholic. In July of that year however, she rescinded her membership in the Church in accordance with strict Party regulations required to marry a man of the SS. Several years after the end of the war, she altered her stance once again by rejoining the Church.

After watching her health deteriorate for more than a decade, Elfriede finally succumbed to her numerous illnesses on December 29th, 1998. Dead at the age of 86, several days later she was mourned by family and friends at a service held at the Pfarrkirche in Alt Aussee. Supported by his two surviving children, Völker and Andrea, a visibly frail Höttl walked behind his wife's flower-draped coffin, as it was escorted from the Church by a group of villagers and laid to rest in the family plot overlooking the lake.

In the first months following Elfriede's funeral, most of Höttl's days were spent holed up in his home at Lichtersberg 194. Perhaps because Elfriede's passing had been so long in coming, he seemed to recover his equilibrium fairly quickly, avoiding the decline in spirit and physical health, common to so many widowed partners. To family and friends gathered to celebrate his eighty-fourth birthday on March 19th, his general state of health appeared sound enough to discount any immediate concerns. Having adjusted to life alone, albeit aided by a part-time housekeeper, his somewhat slowed routine gradually reached a predictable rhythm, and he continued to welcome friends as well as the occasional researcher. In the middle of June however, a chance accident forced the cancellation of all scheduled appointments.

Frau Hofer (Höttl): 2002

"He fell at home and broke the end of his thigh bone. He was operated on and the bone was re-set in the hip joint. He had recovered relatively well and home care had already been organized,… He would have been able to remain at home and someone would come three times a day. That was all organized and then Father fell out of bed at the hospital. After discovering him, they simply put him back in bed. He complained of extreme pain but no action was taken. It was only later that they discovered he had broken the other hip bone in the second fall. He fell on Monday, was transferred to surgery on Wednesday, and he died the following Tuesday… one week after the fall."

Considering the fates that might have befallen an active intelligent operative over the span of his career, the circumstances of Höttl's death on the morning of June 27th,1999, were considerably less dramatic. In the four days between his passing and the scheduled funeral, the past began to catch up with the present as rumours circulated over the number of *"old comrades"* who might come to pay their final respects.

Frau Hofer (Höttl): 2002

"There was one man who came… an old man, bald in a brown suit, who literally stumbled into the Church at the last minute. He pretty much stayed in

the background, but at the cemetery came forward to express his condolences before he disappeared. From the way he looked and behaved I'd have to include him in the category of a former and unrepentant Nazi. But who he was, I have no idea."

Shortly before 2:00 pm on Saturday, July 31st, bells at the Alt Aussee church began to peal, a signal that the cortege bearing Höttl's body was underway from the nearby viewing chapel. Several minutes later, the procession came into view, Hottl's flower-draped casket at the fore, flanked by six honorary pallbearers. Following were family members dressed in black and a group of sympathizers clad in the traditional Tracht of the region, men in jackets and Lederhosen, women in Dirndls. While mourners crowded into the small stone church for the scheduled service, members of a thirty-piece brass band, attired in brown uniforms and matching caps, assembled in the adjacent street, observed by pods of passing tourists. Approximately fifty minutes later, family and friends reemerged into brilliant sunshine to align themselves behind the casket and an honour guard, made up of five elderly men adorned with green and white sashes denoting their Bad Aussee order. As the bells resumed, the procession slowly moved off, the family followed by the men, the separated women bringing up the rear, all to the accompaniment of a traditional burial hymn played by the brass band. Thirty minutes later, and eight-four years after his birth, the man who for much of his life was energized by the concept of making history as opposed to teaching it, was lowered into the ground alongside his wife in a back corner of the lakeside cemetery.

Of all the elements to play a significant role in the final segment of Höttl's life, few had been of more importance to him than the selection of a repository for his 'private papers'. Having often prophesied that future historians would increasingly depend on such documents once the last of the 'Zeitzeugen' were gone, Höttl attempted to guarantee his own chronicles a prominent berth by pledging the entire collection to the Austrian State Archives in Vienna. That commitment was the culmination of his decade long work with Dr. Peter Broucek, who had been instrumental in convincing Höttl of the need to see history preserved. Several months after Höttl's passing, Broucek, who in the interim had become head of the War Archives, traveled to Bad Aussee to inspect the thirty or so boxes stored in the attic of Höttl's daughter-in-law. Prior to that visit, an internal family agreement had designated Höttl's daughter, Andrea, to be responsible for her father's collection. Once his inspection was completed, Broucek announced he was prepared to accept the entire collection.

Following the transfer of the papers to Vienna, familial interest in Höttl's legacy, limited as it was in the first place, began to fade even further. As a result, no one in the family paid much attention when Broucek failed to follow through with his promise of sending the family a detailed table of contents once the papers had been fully appraised and registered. That mutual ambivalence changed in July 2002 when a formal request to examine the papers was submitted by a journalist in Germany. Broucek happened to be on vacation at the time, so responsibility for responding to interested parties had fallen to his secretary, Frau Böhm. Calling to inquire on the status of his request, the journalist was duly informed the collection was closed to public view. Queried as to why, fifty-seven years after the war, the papers had been *"gesperrt"* (closed), Frau Böhm would only go as far as stating they had been deemed 'too sensitive' for public access. Unable or unwilling to offer further details, she inadvertently conceded that to the best of her knowledge, the sealing of the 'noble gentleman's papers', did not apply to family members. Subsequent calls to Völker Höttl and Andrea Hofer, quickly established that no one in the family was aware of the *'Sperrung'*, nor were they adverse to granting access to the files to outside parties. Back in his office one week later, Dr. Broucek found himself fielding inquiries about the inspection request in a face to face meeting with its initiator. Clearly pre-informed about the nature of the visit, Broucek was content to reiterate the message his secretary had delivered a week earlier. Pressed for a clarification as to why someone would donate papers to a public institution only to have them closed for an indeterminate period of time, Broucek admitted the decision to seal the files had been his alone. Asked whether he was obligated, morally, if not legally, to have informed the family of such a decision, Broucek switched tactics, claiming that over their eighteen year friendship, Höttl had repeatedly stipulated his papers would only be passed to the Archives, provided the files be closed. According to Broucek, the rationale behind that proviso was Höttl's desire to protect his family from any 'damaging disclosures and possible lawsuits.'

Broucek: 2002
"He had also wanted to protect his reputation and legacy from those who would use the material to 'twist the facts'."

Asked whether it would not have been easier for Höttl or himself to have simply removed any potentially embarrassing, damaging or contentious files before placing them in the Archives, Broucek declined to answer. Instead, he proclaimed his own reputation was at stake and as a man of his word, he could not and would not, abandon the trust Höttl had placed in him. Rising from his chair to signal an end to the discussion, Broucek was informed that both Höttl's surviving children, were unaware of any specifications attached to the donation, and had agreed to assist in overcoming a ruling they believed had been an arbitrary decision by the Archives. Still on his feet, Broucek launched into a list of requirements he suddenly claimed were compulsory to facilitating such an irregular circumvention of the rules. Confronted with the news Andrea Hofer was prepared to submit a written power of attorney authorizing access, Broucek interrupted his monologue long enough to place a call to Bad Aussee. Despite obvious attempts to have Frau Hofer reconsider, the authorizing fax arrived several minutes later.

Over the next three years, five separate week long visits would be required to inspect the 20,000 documents making up Höttl's papers. Although much of the information proved to be superfluous to that in his SS and NSDAP files, nothing discovered amidst the 'Private papers' implied Broucek's action had in any way been justified.

Joachim Fest: Faces of the Third Reich

"The nucleus of the early membership was a militant minority of the disappointed and embittered of all classes...Many members were inarticulate discontents, men with unbalanced natures, their system of values perverted by the war and the post-war troubles. Many were motivated by the illusions and dreams such as universal yet vague ideas of renewal, or the usurped role of defender against Bolshevism. All impulses of any effectiveness were absorbed into the National Socialist philosophy, which within a certain overall framework, was largely left to its own devices by the leadership. Surprisingly enough, the inconsistency of this philosophy, far from pointing up its essential spuriousness, actually constituted its specific attraction for many intellectuals. By giving free play to all nationalist, conservative or popular revolutionary ideas, it was largely whatever imagination at any given moment demanded of it."

Joachim Fest: Faces of the Third Reich

"Every intellectual knows an occasional temptation to fall for the charlatan. But when the charlatans suddenly appear in droves, and not with the gesture of ironic detachment, but the mien of dark wisdom, then everything points to one of those crises of the spirit that precede politico-moral catastrophes... Such behaviour is more horrifying than the believed idiocies, and reveals something more than the dilemma of a scholarly mind."

Joachim Fest: The Faces of the Third Reich

"The attraction of the NSDAP lay precisely in the fact that it assuaged the need for aggression felt by the masses who had been reduced to despair by defeat, the power vacuum of the post-war years, the inflation and later the world economic crisis."

Q: Why did educated people become Nazis?
Höttl: 1999

"Ya, why not? It was a dream for me. Many, including myself, dreamed that the Reich would one day rise again, not necessarily National Socialist, rather the old Germany where there were proper leaders....The Nazis were a logical continuation from the German Nationalists. This was something I lived and experienced since my childhood in my parents' house. It was simply

logical. At that time one said it was finally the fulfillment of our dream of the union with Germany. The greater German Reich. For intelligent people, and I consider myself to be one, this was seen as something realistic that would come or had to come."

Gitta Sereny:
'Intelligence should not necessarily equated with morality'.

Höttl: 1999
"(Odilo) Globocnik is a good example of what happened to people during the Third Reich. He was born in Trieste, an old Austrian,... the monarchy was there and he grew up with that. He went to school with Jews in Trieste so he should have known better. He was someone who was intelligent enough and educated enough that he knew that it wasn't correct but did it nonetheless because it was his career."

Andrea Hofer (Höttl): 2002
"I think he became a Nazi to make a career... Was he an opportunist?... In certain regards,... yes, I would acknowledge that, no question... But he was never as much of an opportunist as my mother."

Anonymous acquaintance: (Profile article)
"Höttl was the intellectual type Nazi. When something questionable had to be signed, he managed to pass it on to someone else, or he donned a pair of gloves. First so that he wouldn't get dirty, and second so he would leave no fingerprints".

Richard Overy: Author of Interrogations
"Service to a criminal regime, of whatever form, still furthers the objectives of that regime."
... remaining.

Thorsten Querg Article: FORUM
"Those who were not directly involved in the mass murders, like Höttl and Schellenberg, were at the least extensively informed concerning the goals and the carrying out of the Nazi racial fanaticism. Schellenberg received the so called "result reports" of the Einsatzgruppen, in which the number of those

murdered were entered as if it were simple bookkeeping. Höttl learned ever-
ything that he wanted to know from his colleagues, those who had returned
from the 'probation' in the East, not least from his friend, Eichmann. The SD
leader knew the code language. He knew what 'special handling' really
meant."

Elsa Möser: Resident of Alt Aussee 1997
"My father had served on the Eastern Front. Home on leave he told my
mother what he had seen there... of how the SS had shot the Jews, made them
dig their own graves etc. Every soldier knew about it."

Fritz Fischer: Family Friend 1999
"Although Höttl was no innocent bystander, I doubt whether he actually
directed action to deport Jews. But I'm sure he knew what was going on from
the start."

Andrea Hofer (Höttl): 2002
"I believe that he did know what was going on, but felt powerless to alter
the situation. He couldn't take the family overseas, and had already witnessed
the fates of those who chose to refuse further participation, which was usually
a one way ticket to the Eastern Front. But when a neighbour simply disappe-
ars, then another and another... any normal person would have questioned,
what was up?"

Höttl: (Hitler's Helpers G. Knopp)
"'Ausschlactung von den Juden'. We knew that meant extermination."

Q: Do you feel guilty about not having attempted to do anything
against what was happening?
Höttl: 1999
"Yes... I feel guilty... of course... although I did do a lot of things against
it. Of course I couldn't do it openly, I couldn't say this is wrong, you shouldn't
do this ,... I needed to find an excuse... otherwise it would have had no effect.
That the little Höttl there in Vienna said something,... that was of no interest.
...With my status as someone who issued reports I could only say in my foreign
reports that this was damaging our relations with our friends....I didn't always
know who would be reading these reports. ...Whenever there was an

interesting report, ...'for presentation to the Führer', written on the Führer's typewriter with extra large letters because Hitler could not see very well and out of vanity didn't want to wear glasses. ...that was of course the highest that one could achieve. Whether he actually read it or whether or not it helped, that is of course another question. He was the hard one, who under no circumstances wanted to revise his opinion... And that went all the way down the line. The Führer has decided, ... that was the answer whenever anyone presented something. ...There's nothing more to discuss, but this is typical German art, this blind obedience,...."

Erich Ludd: 2000 (Hamburg) HR Program
"I am one of fifty or sixty million German cowards, and therefore it is my opinion, and I regret to say that, Germany may be a nation rich in military heroes, but it is underdeveloped in civil courage."

Q: As a young man you jumped aboard a train bound for the future. When you recognized it was headed for disaster, was it no longer possible to jump off?
Höttl: 1999
"That is something that one fears in regards to every system. I don't want to say cowardice, rather a shortage of civil courage. .... How man thought inwardly, that is another question, but under a dictatorial system, to say that you suddenly don't want any part of it anymore, that meant at the minimum, a loss to your secure existence."

Uwe Timm: In My Brother's Shadow
"They did not have the courage to object, to say 'no'. In Germany, courage often only comes in a group... If there had only been more who had rejected the idea of forging a fine career... things might not have turned out as they did."

Q: And if someone did oppose something openly?
Höttl: 1999
"The first step was always that these people were transferred to the east. They might have had a good position in Vienna or in Berlin and as punishment were transferred to Poland or to Russia, and assigned to fight partisans there. Something life threatening. That was the result of such behaviour, when

someone had opened their mouth. As I said, I wasn't a hero... I think that there had been protestations made from military organizations,... a few officers have told me that circles in the Wehrmacht were very much against these things but could not carry through any of their objections regarding them. I do not think that Hitler would have let himself be influenced by any such objection."

...... after the war.

Col. Telford Taylor (IMT Prosecutor): 1946

"The profession of arms is an honourable one and can be honourably practised. But it is too clear for argument, that a man who commits crimes cannot plead as a defence, that he committed them in a uniform.

French Prime Minister, Vincent Auriol to a German student: 1950

"When you don't forget, it makes it easier for us to forget'.

(Ignatz Bubis interview in Der Spiegel, 30.11.98)

Q: Because you were a member of the SS, it is difficult for the average person to believe that you were an opponent.

Höttl: 1999

"I didn't go along with it for as long. I used the possibilities I had to work against it and as a result came "under the wheels". You see when you had a position such as I did in Berlin, not in the highest ranks but rather in the middle, and then from one day to the next you are downgraded to the rank of a simple private.,... I received enough for my stance.

Höttl: 1999

"For the average citizen it is hard to believe everything that took place during the Third Reich, that so many reasonable people, so many clever people went along for so long ... how can you believe that?"

Völker Höttl: 2001

"Was my father ever involved in criminal activities? I am 99% sure the answer is no, for one reason simply. All sides tried to implicate him. If someone had found something then it would have come out. They all concerned themselves with it, the Austrians, the Hungarians, and the East Germans. Finally even the Americans when he was no longer useful to them, if something was there, it would have come out."

...... justice.

Anonymous:
"As long as any of these men who helped to perpetrate these crimes are still alive, it would be immoral to do nothing. The shame endures not only because of the compassion for the victims and their families, but also because of the disturbing and haunting knowledge of how many went unpunished."

Höttl: 1999
"At that time for we Austrians, we German-Austrians, I trust myself to say that,...my circle of friends grew very large. There isn't even one amongst them who committed a crime."

Norbert Frei: 1997
(Author of Adenauer's Germany & the Nazi Past)
"Those who had never been personally held accountable could consider themselves symbolically exonerated."

Simon Wiesenthal institute report: Vienna 2003
"Austria has failed to convict a Holocaust perpetrator in more than two decades and refuses to establish a special prosecution agency, despite the existence of numerous suspects in the country".

Q: Do you believe that those people who were highly incriminated were justly punished?
Höttl: 1999
"The big decision for the early release of the prisoners came mainly from the Americans. The Americans had this great sentence of 20 years, and then the people were set free after 3 or 4 years. At every opportunity there was an amnesty. The German government protested initially. They were against it. It was only later that the Germans also did it, but at first it was typical American, the grand style. And then of course when the conflict with Russia began, the Americans changed from one day to the next and said we need the Germans as partners and we can't upset them. That was the big turning point, the Russian politics."
Unknown CIC officer 1947: (At Nuremberg)
"Höttl had delivered a sufficient number of Nazi war criminals to the gallows, unbeknownst to his former associates."

Edith Frischmuth (Austrian Resistance Member): 2004

"Höttl betrayed some of his former colleagues to the CIC to save his own skin. He negotiated with them otherwise he wouldn't have been able to walk around free. His testimony reportedly helped to convict Kaltenbrunner and save his own ass... Höttl and Eichmann had been friends. They made a deal that if either one of them were killed, the survivor would take care of the other one's family. A son of Eichmann's apparently visited Höttl during the time he was the director of the school and before Eichmann was captured in 1960."

...... Nazi gold.

Q: "What do you know about the rumours and stories of the Nazi gold?

Höttl: 1999

"It is no secret that a number of leading Nazis deposited gold and money in Switzerland. That was only possible for people who could cross the border. It was very difficult during the war if you didn't have connections to those positions. Unfortunately, I wasn't one of them that had an account there."

Höttl: 1999

"Those who got their hands on this money... there weren't many of them, ...higher placed people in the Third Reich, saw that with this money,... gold,... they could assure their futures and came to the idea that it would be safe in Switzerland, and when the war was over, of course assumed with a Nazi victory, that man could retrieve it. It was a plainly clear speculation...The Swiss are businessmen and throughout the war they earned a lot of money through legal deposits of money and gold Germany made in order to buy important war materials. ...The Swiss banks and the Swedish also earned a fair amount, that is clear......There were several people who saw it as their prime purpose to establish and nurture these connections. They were allowed to travel back and forth. Although not everyone admitted that they were doing it for themselves, it was known that some were making private deposits."

...... traits.

Walter Schellenberg: (Former head of Amt VI) March 1946

"Höttl is a very intelligent man and very industrious in his work. I'm sure in due time he would have made Foreign Office... but Höttl was too easy with his money, spent too much legally and illegally. I always had to keep a strict watch and hold on him. You always had to have him under your supervision."

Edith Frischmuth (Austrian Resistance Member): 1999

"He was a very dangerous person...He knew what was expected from an SS man or an SD man in the Nazi era...He must have been very active to have risen so far so fast...... He only looked out for his own advantage. He was very crafty and impenetrable. You couldn't pin anything on him. But he was a swindler nonetheless."

Q: Was he the kind of man who believed he never made mistakes?
Völker Höttl: 2001

"Yes, absolutely and unequivocally... Eventually he came to the point where he reviewed things and saw that he had made many mistakes. He accepted that and then for him the matter was closed. It was a point where he saw himself as a witness and historian and no longer as an active participant. Then he didn't talk about mistakes he had made, rather he spoke of mistakes in a general sense. The other didn't fit to him. He didn't make any mistakes."

Völker Höttl: March 2000

"There were things he just wouldn't offer up on his own. There were things from the private sphere that I knew about, that he simply suppressed, where he simply claimed 'that was never so.'... When he didn't want something, then it didn't exist. There were areas that he covered up and you could only get a small amount of information out of him. The older he got and the more distance there was from it, he opened up a little. But with him there was always the fear that someone would try to implicate him somehow."

Völker Höttl: 2001

If someone contradicted him... he wasn't used to that. He didn't want it and the whole family regulated itself around that... his mother-in-law thought he was someone who lived in a *"Scheinwelt."* (Dream world)

Frau Hofer (Höttl): 2002

"My father was more open to talk about it than my mother. They were part of a generation who didn't want to talk about it. Basically no one really wanted to talk about it."

Frau Hofer (Höttl): 2002

"He had no hobbies... He was not musical... He claimed to be an avid

admirer of Beethoven and Mozart and had purchased a number of shellac re-
cords... but he never listened to them. We couldn't understand why... He
wasn't a braggart as such, but perhaps there were certain things he felt would
increase his prestige or give him a better image... He collected "kitsch",... espe-
cially as he got older. Plastic items, really tasteless. He did have rugs of some
value. He gave one to his sister, who had it estimated at 10,000 to 15,000 Schil-
lings. ... and model weapons."

...... regrets?

Reinhard Gehlen (Head of OG):
'A good intelligence man never writes about his work, his system or his
service. Because he knows so much, he must take it to his grave.'

Q: Do you share Gehlen's opinion?
Höttl:1999
"No. Myself, I don't have any secrets. I stand for what I did and consider
it correct today that for so long I didn't see through it. Others who were cleverer
than I also didn't. That has to be said. It is so easy to say 'oh they had to have
known'... My stance had always been determined by my anti-Communism. I
can more or less say with satisfaction, that I not only experienced the destruc-
tion of Communism, but also of National Socialism. It is satisfaction enough
to have experienced that and perhaps to have helped a little in that."

◆

Despite massive evidence to the contrary, Höttl's capacity to wallow in
the illusion he had somehow aided in the demise of National Socialism was
unrelenting. He made the claim again in what was to be one of the last interviews ever given. As that three hour discussion drew to a close, Höttl had le-
aned back in a moment of contemplation, his wan and beleaguered face
belying his feigned stamina.

Höttl: 1999
"Yes, ... all what you know of me..."

Not all perhaps, but enough.

COL. BURTON C. ANDRUS – US Army Commander at Nuremberg, during the International Military Tribunal.

BERTA & HANS AUERBOCH – Long time residents of Alt Aussee, who moved to the area shortly after their marriage in 1940. After the war, the forty-two year old Hans worked as a police officer and operative for the CIC.

HILDEGARD BEETZ – Beetz returned to Weimar after the end of hostilities, where she was arrested and taken into custody by American forces. Aware she had kept a diary during her time in Italy, the Americans assigned her the code name *"Felicitas"*, and proceeded to subject their 'valuable catch' to intense interrogation on her detailed knowledge of the inner workings of the RSHA and the names and activities of its various agents.

COUNT FOLKE BERNADOTTE – While working at the Swedish legation's temporary headquarters in Friedrichsrühe, Germany, Bernadotte was summoned to a meeting with Reichsführer Heinrich Himmler in Lübeck. At the meeting on April 24th, 1945, Himmler proposed a complete surrender of German forces to the Allies, providing Germany could continue the fight against Russia. The offer was later rejected by the Allies, but that did not stop Bernadotte from also conducting *"peace negotiations"* with SD leader Walter Schellenberg. Appointed President of the International Red Cross after the war, he became an active mediator in the Palestine conflict. (May 20th 1948) Shortly after submitting a peace plan on September 17th 1948, he and UN Observer Col. Andre P. Serot of the French Air Force were shot and killed in Jerusalem by a members of the Stern gang.

LT. COL. SMITH W. BROOKHART JR. – Born in Iowa, Brookhart was Höttl's chief interrogator at Nuremberg.

JOSEF BÜRKEL – Born 1894 in the Pfalz region of Germany, Bürkel later became the Gauleiter for the area which included the Saarland. He died in September 1944.

WILHELM CANARIS – As Chief of the German Military Intelligence agency,(Abwehr) until it's annexation by the SD, Canaris was arrested and jailed following the failed Hitler assassination plot in July of1944. He was executed by his Nazi captors at the Flossenburg concentration camp in April 1945.

DR. ERNST CHLAN – Born December 24th, 1912, Chlan was the SD sector leader in Vienna prior to Frederick Polte.

CAPT. I.G. DEGNER – The commander of the US troops occupying Alt Aussee in 1945. According to former resistance member, Joseph Grafl, Degner allegedly split portions of the gold found in the garden at the Villa Kerry, with local resistance leader, Albrecht Gaiswinkler. Despite being an American citizen, Degner did not return to the States after his tour of duty, but instead moved to the nearby town of Bad Ischl where he reportedly used some of the illicit funds to open a tourist agency.

JOSEF (SEPP) DIETRICH – As head of Waffen SS Leibstandarte Adolf Hitler in 1933, Dietrich was in charge of commando unit responsible for killing Hitler's rival, Ernst Röhm in 1934. In 1942, Dietrich helped Höttl attain a post as a war reporter following his demotion and transfer to the Waffen SS in Yugoslavia. Tried, convicted and sentenced to life in 1946, Dietrich was released in 1955 and went to work at an advertising agency in Ludwigsburg. Tried and convicted for his role in the Röhm murder in 1957, he was sentenced to 18 months confinement. Active in HIAG, the association known to have aided former members of the Waffen SS, he died in Ludwigsburg in 1966 at the age of 73.

ALLEN WELSH DULLES – According to a section of the *"Elkhorn"* report, the head of the OSS helped transfer portions of his *'clients'* ill-gotten wealth out of Germany before it could be confiscated by the occupying powers. Returning to practise law from 1946 to 1950, he simultaneously acted as an advisor to the American government in the development of the CIA, an agency he subsequently headed from 1953 to 1961. In that position, Dulles was responsible for operations in Iran, as well as the disastrous Bay of Pigs fiasco in Cuba. He was appointed to the Warren Commission in 1964, to investigate the assassination of JFK , the very man who was rumoured to be planning to replace him before his untimely death. Following the Warren Commission Report, Dulles withdrew from the public spotlight, passing away in Washington D.C. on January 29th, 1969.

LEOPOLD FIGL – Austrian Federal Chancellor from December 12th, 1945 until October 10th, 1952, who also served as Foreign Minister following the granting of Austrian independence in 1955.

EDITH FRISCHMUTH-HAUER – A former Austrian resistance fighter, who was familiar with Höttl's role in the months running up to the German surrender, as well as his multi-faceted career after the war. A feisty outspoken woman, Frischmuth passed away in Alt Aussee in 2004.

THEO GAHRMANN – Born March 3rd.1910, Gahrmann was the SD section leader in Linz.

ALBRECHT GAISWINKLER – In the 1930's, Gaiswinkler reportedly worked for the regional Medical Insurance Board in Bad Aussee. Although married at the time, he apparently began an affair with the director's daughter. As a partial solution to the ensuing scandal, he signed up with the NSDAP and was sent off to serve in the German Army. Captured in France, he was handed over to British authorities who allegedly *"turned"* him to fight the Nazis in his native Austria. After local resident Hans Pucher discovered gold bars in the garden of the Villa Kerry in May 1945, he first reported the find to Gaiswinkler. Instead of turning it over to the Americans, Gaiswinkler reportedly made arrangements for the box to be taken to the home of fellow parachutist, Karl Lietzke for safekeeping. Once matters cooled down and he no longer felt authorities likely to search his own residence, he was thought to have retrieved the box, splitting the contents with the US commander Capt.I.G. Degner. Gaiswinkler was believed to have used his share of the money to build a house in Graz for his former mistress with whom he resumed a relationship after the war.

EDMUND GLAISE-HORSTENAU – Appointed by Hitler as Austrian *"Minister for National Freedom"* just prior to the Anschluss, Glaise-Horstenau was later made a member of the Council at the German Historical Institute. He reportedly served briefly as a CIC recruit with the code name *"Glore"* before reportedly committing suicide on July 20th 1946, while being held at the Langwasser prisoner-of-war camp near Nuremberg.

ODILO GLOBOCNIK – Reported to have surfaced briefly in Alt Aussee in early 1945, most historians believe Globocnik committed suicide on June 6th, 1945 as he was about to be arrested by a British patrol. Höttl however, claimed this *"realistic thinking person"* did not kill himself but in fact was handed over to the CIC by the British after they declared him dead by his own hand on May 31st, 1945. According to Höttl, Globocnik had continued to work secretly for the CIC for some time.

JOSEF GRAFL – An Austrian resistance fighter, who once described Höttl as a slippery individual that always stayed in the shadows, Grafl was parachuted into Ausseerland in April 1945, along with Albrecht Gaiswinkler and two others. Interviewed in 2006, the 85 year old Grafl claimed a number of metal cases, thought to be have been dumped in the Toplitzsee by fleeing Nazis, had in fact turned up empty on the fields at nearby Wienen in early 1946.

KURT GRIMM – Head of the Austrian resistance in Switzerland, Grimm worked as director of a large Viennese bank. He reportedly attended the meeting held between Höttl and American officials in March 1945.

HEINRICH HIMMLER – Appointed Reichsführer SS in 1929, Himmler became Police President of Munich in 1933. On April 20th, 1934 Hitler appointed his faithful ally, Deputy Chief of the Secret Police in Prussia. By 1936 Himmler had risen to be Chief of the entire German police network. At a conference of assembled Gauleitern and Reichleitern in Posen on Oct. 6th, 1943, Himmler revealed details of the Final Solution now in progress, commending members of his audience for their stamina to see the *"extermination of the Jews"* through to its end.

Höttl
"Himmler was as he looked. He was, as we say in German, a petty bureaucrat. He was everything else but a personality, not only in the way he looked but in every manner. He had the luck that as a true servant of his master, he rose along with Hitler. He was a very good organizer. When he

saw that something was successful he responded accordingly and in doing so garnered a lot of important people for the SS, which ultimately led to the power of the SS. He couldn't have done that on his own. Heydrich was the main figure, the rising star. He wasn't like Himmler, who presented himself in the foreground. He was the large figure who worked behind the scenes. Almost no one knew anything about Heydrich, that he was the one pulling the strings. He wouldn't have only replaced Himmler, he also toyed with the idea of replacing Hitler."

ANDREA HOFER – Höttl's third child and only daughter. Now retired, she and her husband Fritz Hofer live in Bad Aussee.

GERTRUDE HÖTTL – Reportedly a strong supporter of the Nazis as well as a dues paying member of the illegal NSDAP, Höttl's sister worked as an accountant/auditor for several firms in Vienna. She is believed to have died from leukaemia in the early 1990's.

HAGEN HÖTTL – As Höttl's first born son, Hagen reportedly bore the brunt of his father's expectations to follow him into an academic career. Said to have been less ambitious than his father wanted, Hagen instead settled down to a quiet life in Bad Aussee, raising two children with his wife Helga Ludwig, a pharmacist's daughter whom he met while attending school. Shunning life further afield, he remained in Bad Aussee, working as a sales representative for a pharmaceutical firm before passing away in 1992 after a long battle with cancer.

Völker Höttl

"Hagen for the most part was a good natured person, and an unbelievably laid back person. He was very similar to my grandfather on my mother's side. On one hand he never wanted to rub someone the wrong way, and on the other always wanted to be left in peace. And he let almost everyone dump on him. Also my father… he noticed this. He had practically no chance to convince him of anything. It began with the simplest of things, with household chores, where he stood around looking dumb, so that people would ultimately say "hands off". Nothing motivated him. And this bothered my father. He felt that it was his fault that he didn't amount to much."

HANS HÖTTL – Wilhelm's older brother. Reportedly a reserved individual and not as ardent a follower of the Nazis as his siblings, Hans served somewhere on the front. After the war, he took a job for a meat delivery service before winding his way through a series of other jobs. He later moved to Vienna to work as a sales representative, passing away there in 1998.

HILDEGARDE HÖTTL – Born in 1905, Höttl's eldest sister worked as a civil servant before moving on to the Continuing Board of Education in Vienna. Said to have been a strong Nazi supporter, she reportedly remained such until her death in 1999.

VÖLKER HÖTTL – Höttl's second son. A historian with a Dr. of Philosophy like his father, Völker attended the University of Vienna, completing his doctoral thesis in 1967. Employed with IBM, he lived for a number of years in Cologne with his wife, the daughter of the former Graz Opera director Kojetinsky, and their two children. Following a divorce he moved to a suburb of Düsseldorf with a new partner.

THEODOR INNITZER – The Cardinal of Vienna who wavered between support and criticism of the Nazis. Innitzer died in Vienna on October 9th, 1955.

RUPERT KAIN – Oberbürgermeister (Mayor) of Alt Aussee at the time of the German surrender, Kain was an early NSDAP member, and good friend of regional Gauleiter, August Eigruber. Following his capture by the partisans he was turned over to the US Forces.

ERNST KALTENBRUNNER – Son of an Austrian lawyer, Kaltenbrunner obtained his own law degree in 1929 and began to practise law in Linz. Joining the NSDAP in 1932 he was involved in the attempted putsch of July 1934. Tried and found guilty of treason, he was jailed by Austrian authorities. Following his release in 1935, he went on to play a leading role in co-ordinating the illegal NSDAP in Austria. Made a Brigadier General after the Anschluss in 1938, Kaltenbrunner was appointed State Secretary for Security in 1939. Promoted to Lieutenant General of the Police in Vienna in 1942, he was selected to take over as head of the RSHA in January 1943. According to Amt VI leader Walter Schellenberg, Kaltenbrunner was responsible for a myriad of crimes, not the least of which were the notorious death marches. Himmler reportedly wanted to leave the concentration camps and their inmates intact, but it was Kaltenbrunner who managed to persuade Hitler to act otherwise. Tried, convicted, and sentenced to death at Nuremberg, he was hanged on Oct. 16th, 1946.

FRITZ KAUDERS – Theories about Richard *"Fritz"* Kauders' true identity abound. The most prominent claimed his real name was Richard Klatt, born June 23rd 1903 in Vienna. A trained construction engineer, who happened to be Jewish, Klatt allegedly fled Austria after the Anschluss to what he thought would be a safe haven in Hungary. Arrested and handed over to German border police in 1940, he avoided being sent to a concentration camp through the help of an acquaintance who worked for the Abwehr. Allowed to return to Hungary, he began to travel to various south eastern European countries, raising speculation that *"Major"*, his alleged codename, was working for the SD. Allegedly caught trying to entice a Gestapo agent into trading intelligence information, he was arrested in Agram (Zagreb) on Sept. 24, 1941, on orders of the RHSA. Charged with treason, carrying false identity papers and breaking the race code, he was subjected to intense interrogation by the regional police in Vienna, before telling authorities he had been in Yugoslavia on assignment for Höttl. The ensuing investigation reportedly exposed him as *"Max,"* one of the most valued agents in south eastern Europe, with ties deep within Russian political circles. In 1942, Kauders fell under the suspicion of an Abwehr operative by the name of Capt. Otto Wagner alias *"Dr. Delius"*, who accused him of being a Soviet double agent. Using his influence with Abwehr chief Wilhelm Canaris, Wagner tried to see Kauders was sent to a concentration camp. More interested in gaining information from Kauders' alleged contacts than seeing him jailed, Canaris was able to forestall the transfer. Despite a belated attempt by Höttl to secure the freedom of his one time protege, sources suggest Kauders eventually was sent to Auschwitz, dying there on January 12th, 1943.

WILHELM FREIHERR von KETTELER – Von Ketteler was murdered in March or April of 1938, while serving as attaché at the German Embassy in Vienna. Twenty four years later, Höttl was summoned by a Düsseldorf court to testify about his knowledge and possible role in the crime.

DORIS KOCHS – Believed to have been one of Höttl's private secretaries.

RICHARD KORHERR – Himmler's SS Inspector for Statistics, assigned to review Eichmann's estimates of Jewish deaths after Himmler considered the number too low.

JACOB LEVY – A Jewish born native of Breslau, Levy worked as a jeweller in his home city as well as Berlin, before being forced to flee to Switzerland in the mid 1930's. He re-surfaced in Budapest in 1944, equipped with a Dutch passport in the name of Jaac van Haarten. In possession of a substantial amount of money reported to have come from trading art works for Red Cross transit visas, van Haarten was active in rescuing threatened Jews in Hungary. An indication of the level of contacts van Haarten is thought to have had, on April 26th 1945, he was authorized by Kaltenbrunner to obtain the release of numerous Jews for use as a goodwill gesture for Höttl's final talks in Switzerland. Other sources claim van Haarten was also an agent for Operation Bernhard's distribution network.

KONRAD LIENHART – As head of Swiss Intelligence for the St. Gallen region in Switzerland, Lienhart helped arrange for Höttl to meet with US officials in February,1945.

DR. JOSEF LÖWENHERZ – The Executive Director of the Vienna Jewish Community, whose office was forced to deliver weekly reports on the progress of Jewish emigration to Eichmann. The same reports were known to have passed across Höttl's desk.

JOHN J.(ay) McCLOY – Born March 31,1895 in Philadelphia, McCloy was a lawyer and diplomat as well as an advisor to every President from Roosevelt to Reagan. Appointed Assistant Secretary of War in 1941, he was later criticized for opposing plans to bomb the railroads leading to Auschwitz. Between 1947 and 1949 he was President of the World Bank. From 1949 to 1952 he served as High Commissioner to Germany, during which time he helped create a civilian government and establish a base for Germany's reconstruction. He also oversaw the general amnesty granted to many of the war criminals. Like Allen Dulles, McCloy was also later appointed a member of the Warren Commission. He died on March 11, 1989 in Stamford, Connecticut.

HEINRICH MÜLLER – Born in Munich in 1900, Müller trained as an airplane mechanic and served during the First World War before entering the service of the Munich police in 1919. Appointed Senior Police Secretary in 1933, he joined the SS in April 1934, and was later transferred to the State Secret Police in Berlin. Due to his association with the Bavarian State Police, there were grave misgivings about letting Müller join the Party. As a result he didn't officially join the NSDAP until 1939. From that point until his disappearance in early 1945, he headed the notorious Amt IV, the department responsible for overseeing the investigation of perceived enemies of the State. As head of the Gestapo, he was also one of the main participants at the Wannsee Conference in January 1942, called to solidify steps for the *"Final Solution"*.

CAJETAN MÜHLMANN – After attaining a Ph.D in art history in the mid 1920's, Mühlmann established himself as a well known art critic and author in Austria. Appointed chief publicity officer for the Salzburg Festival in 1926, he made a point of cultivating numerous friendships early in his career. Included in that calculated coterie were the sisters of Hermann Göring, both of whom lived near Salzburg, as well as the SS Gauleiter, Odilo Globocnik. Mühlmann also managed to form a close alliance with the lawyer Arthur Seyss-Inquart, and in 1934 the pair began working for the interests of the Nazi Party in Austria. Moving to Germany a short while later, he reportedly became an agent for Reinhard Heydrich, playing both sides of the political fence by ferrying shipments of illegal propaganda and weapons into Austria in return for sensitive information he reportedly delivered to a high ranking official in Hitler's Chancellory. Following the Anschluss, Mühlmann was able to take advantage of his many friendships to reap the benefits of the Aryanization program underway in Austria. Residing in an apartment in Vienna's Schloss Belvedere, while working out of a Nazi-confiscated office on the adjacent Prinz Eugen Str., Mühlmann furnished both dwellings with confiscated luxury items obtained through the Nazi VUGESTA program. During this stint in Vienna, he was given responsibility for overseeing the collection of artworks confiscated from Austrian Jews. As a result of that experience, in 1939 Reichsmarshall Hermann Göring assigned Mühl-mann to the task of *"securing"* artwork taken from Jews recently sent to territories in newly conquered Poland. The following year he was reques-ted to apply those same talents to South Tyrol. Leaders in northern Italy however, were reluctant to accept terms of Mühlmann's appointment, managing to stall long enough until he was re-assigned to Holland, then under the jurisdiction of his friend, Seyss-Inquart. Captured by the Ame-ricans on June 15th, 1945, Mühlmann was interrogated by the CIC at Camp Markus in Western Austria. Persuaded to expound on the activi-ties of his former friends, his testimony eventually helped convict many of those men at Nuremberg. Returned to Austrian authorities in Oct.1946, he found himself facing a extradition order issued by the Polish govern-ment. Due to a law passed in the summer of 1947 however, which restric-ted extradition of suspected war criminals of Austrian descent, Mühl-mann was able to avoid facing a Polish court. American Military authorities subsequently quashed the *"new Law"*, but Austrian officials still declined to hand him over, claiming they had no idea as to his whe-reabouts despite the fact he was in an SS internment camp serving out a two year sentence for membership in that organization. Shipped back to Germany on August 18th, 1947, Mühlmann was placed in the custody of the Military Government of Bavaria. He escaped in February 1948, living quietly in a suburb of Munich until 1952, when Austrian authorities brought charges of high treason against him. Languishing between the two court systems for years, the 60 year old Mühlmann died of cancer on August 2nd 1958.

BENITO MUSSOLINI – The Italian Fascist leader and Hitler's Axis partner was executed on April 28, 1945. The next day, German troops in Italy formerly surrendered as part of Operation Sunrise, negotiated by Karl Wolff and Allen Dulles.

ALFRED NAUJOCKS – The SS officer who technically *"started"* the Second World War, Naujocks reportedly defected to the Americans in October 1944. Interned briefly as a witness at Nuremberg, he moved to Hamburg after his release to work as a businessman. Never required to face a court of law for his numerous wartime activities, Naujocks passed away in April of 1966.

DR. KARL NEY – Reportedly a sporadic SD agent in Budapest, in October 1944, Ney worked in conjunction with Otto Skorzeny and Erich Kernmayer to establish an information network in areas of Hungary about to be overrun by the Soviets. After the war, he was said to have made his services available to Reinhard Gehlen, later working for the German Intelligence Agency, BND.

IVER OLSON – An American member of the War Refugee Board, Olson was credited with having recruited Raoul Wallenberg to assist in rescue efforts in Hungary in 1944. Olson had also been an accountant with the OSS in Sweden, leading some sources to believe the Soviets suspected Wallenberg was engaging in espionage against them. Shortly after the war, Wallenberg disappeared while en route to a meeting with Russian officials.

GRÄFIN DOROTHY PALFFY – Höttl's first trip to Alt Aussee in 1939, was reportedly made to arrange for Austrian passports for Palffy's persecuted relatives in Poland. After an extended stay in Alt Aussee, during which time she reportedly resided at the home of then Mayor Kalss, the American countess returned to the US after the war.

GRAF FIDEL PALFFY – No relation to Dorothy Palffy. As the leader of a right wing Party in Hungarian politics in the 1940's, Palffy became Agricultural Minister in the Arrow Cross Cabinet of his competitor Ferenc Szalasi. Thought to have been a close contact of Höttl's, he was hanged for treason in March of 1946.

OTTOKAR PESSL – Born 21.8.1913, Pessl was Höttl's driver throughout most of his career in the SD, a trade he continued to ply after the war.

JULIUS RAAB – Austrian Chancellor from 1953 to 1964, and Höttl's occasional walking companion when vacationing in Alt Aussee.

DR. FRIEDRICH RAINER – Born in the Austrian State of Carinthia in 1903, Rainer joined the NSDAP in 1930 and SS in 1934. Arrested and jailed for high treason in 1935, the trained lawyer was appointed head of the provincial government in Salzburg in 1938, before eventually moving on to become an SS Lieutenant General and Gauleiter over his native district of Carinthia in 1941. Captured in May 1945, he was brought to Nuremberg to testify as a crown witness against the likes of Seyss-Inquart. Extradited to Yugoslavia in Feb. 1947, *'Friedl'* was convicted of wartime activities and executed in Ljubljana in July of that year.

DR. OTTO RASCH – SS Brigadier General and Inspector in the SD, Rasch reportedly had a fierce row with Höttl in 1941 over the latter's unauthorized work in foreign countries. Höttl claimed to have soothed nerves in Berlin headquarters shortly before Rasch was assigned to head Einsatzgruppe C in October that same year. Charged after the war for his complicity in those activities, plans for his prosecution were staid due to his ill health. Rasch died in November of 1948.

HEINZ REITH – Employed as Hausmeister at Höttl's school, Reith also worked occasionally as his driver after the war. He was also involved in an aborted diving expedition at the Topltzsee.

DR. ANDREAS ROHRACHER – As Archbishop of Salzburg from 1943 until 1969, he reportedly endorsed the *"Austria Group's"* plans to seek a separate peace with the Western Allies in early 1945. After the war, Rohracher joined the chorus calling for the amnesty of war criminals, warning that proposed anti-Nazi legislation would only succeed in creating a bastion of martyrs.

IRIS SCHEIDLER – Born Iris Jockl, the wife of Kaltenbrunner's adjutant and good friend of Elfriede Höttl, is thought to have remarried after the war. She remained in contact with Höttl until at least 1988, but reports she committed suicide in Berlin could not be confirmed.

WALTER SCHELLENBERG – The former head of Amt VI, Schellenberg was actively involved in peace negotiations with Abraham Steven Hewitt, an advisor to US President Roosevelt, and the Swedish diplomat Count Bernadotte. He was reportedly staying at Bernadotte's private residence at the time of the German surrender, and remained there until June 17th, when he flew to Frankfurt to surrender to authorities. Initially transferred to London for interrogation, he was later sent to Nuremberg to give testimony to the International Tribunal. Höttl claimed his former boss managed to have all his sensitive files put on to microfilm and buried in a secret location in Berlin before the German collapse. Other sources support that version but claim the microfilm was destroyed during Schellenberg's absence in March of 1945. Despite Höttl's earlier urgings to 'tell all', few of Schellenberg's secrets ended up in his memoir, The Labyrinth, published posthumously in 1957.

ARTUR SEYSS-INQUART – Reich Governor of the Ostmark until April 30th 1939, Seyss-Inquart was made Reichsminister without Portfolio the following day. Five months later he was re-assigned to Cracow as a Higher SS leader and deputy to Poland area leader Hans Frank. Seyss-Inquart's career later took him to Holland, where he participated in the deportation of thousand of Dutch Jews. Amongst the top Nazis leaders found guilty at the International Military Tribunal in Nuremberg, he was hanged on Oct. 16th, 1946.

FRANZ SIX – Labelled by Eichmann as *"an eager beaver"*, when it came to the genocide of the Jews, the SS Brigadier General was sentenced in 1948 to 20 years for crimes committed with a special commando unit in Einsatzgruppe B. Released from Landsberg prison in 1952, he worked briefly for the Gehlen Operation before eventually finding employment in a publishing house in Darmstadt. Over the next decade, he would wade through a series of jobs in various German cities before moving to South Tyrol. Six died in Bozen in July 1975 at the age of 69.

FRANZ STANGL – Born on March 26th, 1908 in Altmunster, Austria, Stangl worked as a policeman in the city of Wels while his interest in the Nazi movement gradually developed. Although he claimed to have joined the illegal Austrian NSDAP in 1936 in order to protect himself, Stangl's sister-in-law Helene Eidenbrock, stated he became a member largely because it was the illegals who *"got on"* in their careers. Made an official of the Jewish Referat for the Linz Gestapo in 1938, Stangl was appointed Director of the Nazi euthanasia unit at Hartheim in 1940. Based on his experience at that institution, he was later made Commandant of the extermination camps at Sóbibor and Treblinka. Able to escape captivity in Linz in 1948, he fled to Brazil via Syria. Captured in 1967, he went on trial in Düsseldorf in 1970. Convicted and sentenced to life, he died in prison in June 1971.

DR. LEOPOLD TAVS – Born in Budweis in the Sudentenland, on July 7th, 1898, Tavs had already received his Engineer's Diploma by the time he joined the NSDAP in January 1931. Appointed as the *"unofficial"* Gauleiter of Vienna in 1937, he was arrested and jailed after Austrian officials raided the offices of a Nazi committee and discovered plans for a putsch plot against the government. Rather than being punished for his alleged crimes, Tavs was transported to Berlin where he was made a ministerial Secretary and a regional co-ordinator for the Party. Returning to Vienna in May of 1939, he took up a post as Director of the Municipal Housing Department, before eventually being elected city councillor in March of 1941. After brief service in the Army in late 1942, he was sent to work at the Daimler-Puch factory in Steyr. By May 1943 Tavs was back with the Wehrmacht, a posting he retained until the end of the war. He passed away in Vienna in December of 1985.

ADRIAN von FÖLKERSAM – Otto Skorzeny's Chief of Staff and military brain, the SS Captain was active in planning various operations, including Operation Panzerfaust, the code name given to the overthrow of the Hungarian Regent, Admiral Horthy in 1944.

KURT von HALLER – An employee of German Military Intelligence (Abwehr) until Nazi Foreign Office diplomat Edmund Veesenmayer recruited him to work as an aide to State Secretary Wilhelm Ketteler. Von Haller served as part of the German legation in Budapest in 1944, during which time he became a close colleague of Höttl.

BALDUR von SCHIRACH – A native of Berlin, von Schirach belonged to the inner circle of Hitler's trusted aides as far back as 1925. Persuaded to join the NSDAP leadership in 1928, he was later responsible for founding and expanding the Hitler Youth, an organization he claimed provided *"unlimited opportunities for children from poor circumstances "*. With slogans such as *"Youth leading youth"* and organized activities that included hiking, bike tours, sport, music, and comradeship, the HJ appealed to thousands of young Germans and Austrians, who were not overly concerned with the more doctrinal aspects of the organization. Serving as Gauleiter of Vienna from 1940 until it's seizure by the Russians, von Schirach was captured in June of 1945. Sentenced to 20 years at

Nuremberg, he was one of the few Nazis who actually served out his full sentence. Released from Spandau prison in September 1966, he lived another eight years before dying in the late summer of 1974.

GERO von SCHULZE GÄVERNITZ – A German-born American, who was a top assistant to OSS leader Allen Dulles in Bern.

HEINRICH RITTER von SRBIK – One of Höttl's professors at the University of Vienna, Srbik was quoted as having viewed Austria's union with Germany as a *"unifying experience"*. Appointed President of the German Historical Commission, he went on to serve as President of the Academy of Sciences in Vienna. Believed to have received the Goethe Medallion for Art and Science from Hitler himself in 1944, von Srbik retired to Tyrol after the war, where he continued to publish his writings up until his death in February 1951.

MAXIMILIAN FREIHERR von WEICHS – The Field Marshal in charge of implementing the Nazi plan to occupy Hungary in March of 1944, (Operation Margarethe) von Weichs was later responsible for the internal security of that country. Although ostensibly head of the Army command, he was not allowed to place direct demands upon the Horthy government without first receiving permission from Ambassador Veesenmayer and the military attache, General Hans V. Greiffenberg. Charged in a 1948 court case investigating the murder of civilians in south eastern Europe, von Weichs was released due to his poor health, dying on September 27th, 1954.

ERNST FREIHERR von WEIZSÄCKER – As the former German Ambassador to the Vatican, von Weizsäcker was put on trial as part of the Minister's Process in 1949. Sentenced to seven years he was released in 1950, living in Lindau until his death on August 5th 1951.

FRITZ WESTEN – The Austrian entrepreneur's death in 1951 allegedly caused Höttl to suffer a nervous breakdown. Westen was involved in a number of shadowy business adventures after the war. Amongst his reputed exploits was a spell as agent # 503 for the OSS.

GUIDO ZIMMER – Born Nov. 18th 1911 in the German town of Bür, Zimmer joined the NSDAP in 1932. After officially entering SS and SD ranks in 1936, he moved to the Foreign Intelligence sector of the RSHA in 1940. The Italian Referat at the time of the Allied invasion of southern Italy in September 1943,he was later involved with Höttl in establishing a network of agents who could supply the Nazis with intelligence if the Allies overran the country. Also linked to the persecution and deportations of of Jews in Genoa and Milan, Zimmer initiated contacts with Allied intelligence in November 1944, regarding a possible surrender of German troops. As a result of his *'usefulness'* in those negotiations, he reportedly later received protection from prosecution from Allen Dulles. Despite Höttl's claim that his *"Italian representative"* had fled to South America after the war, CIA name files show that Zimmer remained in Europe working as a secretary with Italian businessman Baron Luigi Parrilli, while freelancing with the OSS. Following his contact with the Gehlen Organization in 1948, he renewed ties with a number of former SS officers in 1950, and remained enmeshed in espionage activities throughout the remainder of that decade.

All SS members had their blood type tattooed under their left armpit to facilitate transfusions following severe injuries.

The record of racial origin, the Sippenbuch, was carried by all members of the SS.

On March 24th,1933, some three months after Hitler's rise to power, the Nazis tried to apply economic pressure on their neighbour's lucrative tourism industry by imposing a 1000RM fine on anyone travelling to Austria.

During twelve years of Nazi reign, over 20 million people were killed… Jews, Communists, Slavs, handicapped, gypsies, and eastern Europeans. Over that same period, 24,000 support camps were built and maintained within the Reich.

'The Jews were merely the first step in the Nazi plan to eradicate all the *"inferior"* races of Europe and Asia.'

There was no separate budget for the planned destruction. Tickets for deportees were booked on the German Rail Network through the Middle European Travel Agency and paid for with money from goods confiscated from the Jews. Charter rates were offered for *"passengers"* being transferred to Auschwitz, with a rebate offered for groups numbering over 400 people. The SS was billed for extra cleaning and damage incurred to rail cars used on the transport trains. – Raoul Hilberg

Forty percent of the staff in the extermination camps were Austrian, despite the fact Austrians made up only eight percent of the total Reich population.

After the arrival of a transport, men were always gassed first to reduce the chance of an uprising. In the early period, arrivals who survived the selection at Birkenau were tattooed on their chest. It was only later identification numbers were tattooed on their forearm.

The idea of killing all the Sonderkommandos after they had spent a specific amount of time carrying out their duties in the extermination camps arose from Reinhard Heydrich. The RSHA leader boasted of having taken the plan from the Pharaohs who ordered the deaths of all those who helped build the pyramids.

"*Melmer*" was the name of the Reichsbank account used for storing Holocaust gold, named after SS Captain Bruno Melmer, who apparently delivered the shipments to the bank.

On December 21, 1942, Monseigneur Kazimierz Papee, the Polish Ambassador to the Vatican from 1939 until 1958, handed a letter to Cardinal Tardini, a top aide to Pope Pius XII, that clearly spelled out the extent of the mass murders occurring in Poland. Shortly before his execution on October 10th, 1946, former Governor of Poland, Hans Frank predicted that "*A thousand years will pass and the guilt of Germany will not be erased*".

The White Rose resistance movement in Germany, whose members included Hans and Sophie Scholl were betrayed at the University of Munich. Charged with having written and distributed anti-Fascist leaflets, they were executed by the Nazis in 1943.

Twelve trials were held in Nuremberg over several years. With the exception of the war crimes trial, all were carried out under the auspices of the Americans. Lawyers, judges, doctors, businessmen, civil servants and industrialists who served the Nazi regime were called to answer for their activities. The 11th trial, known as the Wilhelmstrasse trial, tried four Ministers, seven State Secretaries and numerous high ranking civil servants. Nearly all received early releases and went on to resume their civilian career.

The Republic of Germany failed to formally recognize the verdicts handed down at Nuremberg, and in the 1950's, passed a series of laws that virtually prevented any further prosecutions against bureaucrats who had worked in the RHSA. After West German authorities assumed control of prosecutions from the Allies, only 900 out of some 500,000 Nazis were convicted of crimes. In mid-2015, a review conducted by the '*Zentrale Stelle der Landesjustizverwaltungen zur Aufklärung nationalsozialistischer Verbrechen*' in Ludwigsburg produced a list of 30 perpetrators. Of that number, only six were still considered capable of being brought to trial.

After the war, the son of the businessman whose company delivered Zyklon B to the Nazis, purchased property in and around the Blaa-Alm.

The Toplitzsee diving expedition funded by the Austrian government in 1963, reportedly turned up 38 boxes of material. Some contained fake English pounds. The contents of the others were never fully revealed.

Nazi – allied veterans from lands like Latvia, Lithuania, etc. received pensions for their wartime service to the Nazis, while the majority of Nazi victims in those countries received nothing.

On Dec. 17,1999, the German government announced a settlement with German industry to establish a fund to compensate slave labours who had toiled under atrocious conditions for various German companies during WWII. Of the approximately 2000 companies that benefitted from the slave labour, including such renowned names as Siemens, VW, Daimler, Krupp, Höchst, AEG, Audi, I.G. Farben, and BMW, only 60 came forward to contribute to the fund, some of those only under the threat of American boycotts of their products.

www.ingramcontent.com/pod-product-compliance
Lightning Source LLC
Chambersburg PA
CBHW020242130626
46549CB00005B/2018